G000089503

Hg2 Almaty & Astana

A Hedonist's guide to

Almaty & Astana

Written and photographed by
Summer Coish and Lucy Kelaart

A Hedonist's guide to Almaty & Astana

Managing director – Tremayne Carew Pole
Marketing director – Sara Townsend
Series editor – Catherine Blake
Design – Katy Platt
Maps – Amber Sheers
Repro – Advance Digital Printing
Printers – Printed in Italy by Printer Trento srl
Publisher – Filmer Ltd

Email – info@hg2.com
Website – www.hg2.com

First published in the United Kingdom in November 2007 by
Filmer Ltd
47 Filmer Road
London SW6 7JJ

All rights reserved. No part of this publication may be reproduced or
transmitted in any form or by any means, electronic or mechanical,
including photocopy, recording or any other information storage and
retrieval system without prior permission in writing from the
publisher.

ISBN – 978-1-905428-21-2

Hg2 Almaty & Astana

CONTENTS

How to…

A Hedonist's guide to… is broken down into easy to use sections:
Sleep, Eat, Drink, Snack, Party, Culture, Shop, Play and Info. In each of
these sections you will find detailed reviews and photographs. At the
front of the book you will find an introduction to the city and an
overview map, followed by introductions to the four main areas and
more detailed maps. On each of these maps you will see the places
that we have reviewed, laid out by section, highlighted on the map with
a symbol and a number. To find out about a particular place simply
turn to the relevant section, where all entries are listed alphabetically.
Alternatively, browse through a specific section (e.g. Eat) until you find
a restaurant that you like the look of. Next to your choice will be a
coloured border – each colour refers to a particular area of the city.
Simply turn to the relevant map to discover the location.

Updates

Hg2 has developed a network of journalists in each city to review the
best hotels, restaurants, bars, clubs, etc., and to keep track of the latest
developments – new places open up all the time, while others simply
fade away or just go out of style. To access our free updates as well as
the content of each guide, simply log on to our website www.hg2.com
and register. We welcome your help. If you have any comments or
recommendations, please feel free to email us at info@hg2.com.

Book your hotel on Hg2.com

We believe that the key to a great city break is choosing the right
hotel. Our unique site now enables you to browse through our selection of hotels, using the interactive maps to give you a good feel for
the area as well as the nearby restaurants, bars, sights, etc., before you

book. Hg2 has formed partnerships with the hotels featured in our guide to bring them to readers at the lowest possible price. Our site now incorporates special offers from selected hotels, as well as a diary of interesting events taking place, 'Inspire Me'.

The concept

A Hedonist's guide to... is designed to appeal to a more urbane and stylish traveller. The kind of traveller who is interested in gourmet food, elegant hotels and seriously chic bars – the traveller who feels the need to explore, shop and pamper themselves away from the crowds.

Our aim is to give you an insider's knowledge of a city, to make you feel like a well-heeled, sophisticated local and to take you to the most fashionable places in town to rub shoulders with the local glitterati.

In today's world work rules our life, and weekends away are few and far between; when we do manage to get away we want to have as much fun and to relax as much as possible with the minimum amount of stress. This guide is all about maximizing time. There is a photograph of each place we feature, so before you go you know exactly what you are getting into; choose a restaurant or bar that suits you and your needs.

We pride ourselves on our independence and our integrity. We eat in all the restaurants, drink in all the bars and go wild in the nightclubs – all totally incognito. We charge no one for the privilege of appearing in the guide, and every place is reviewed and included at our discretion.

We feel cities are best enjoyed by soaking up the atmosphere: wander the streets, indulge in some retail therapy, re-energize yourself with a massage and then get ready to eat like a king and party hard on the local scene.

Almaty

Nestled in the foothills of the Zhailiskii Alatau Mountains, part of the great Tien Shan range, which cross Central Asia from east to west, Almaty's location is its greatest asset. The natural mountain scenery provides both a dramatic backdrop and easily accessible playground for the city's one and a half million residents.

In its present form, Almaty (which translates as 'Grandfather of the Apples', in reference to Almaty's numerous fruit-bearing orchards) was established in the mid-nineteenth century when the Russians built a fort at Verniy near the site of a long-established nomadic settlement. As the Russian intent in Central Asia changed from protection to colonization, a small town was established adjacent to the fort.

Subsequent development in the Soviet period turned Almaty (then Alma-Ata) into a thriving capital city with some of its most impressive buildings emerging under the leadership of Dinmukhamed Kunayev, first secretary of Kazakhstan's Communist Party from 1959 to 1986.

In 1997, six years after Kazakhstan gained independence, President Nazarbayev announced his decision to move the capital to Astana in northern Kazakhstan. One of the reasons he cited for leaving was Almaty's location on a major earthquake faultline. Many thought that the move of the capital would prove a death knell for Almaty, but instead the city's popularity has continued to grow and it is now set to become the regional financial hub for all of Central Asia as well as being the country's business and cultural centre. The enormous oil, gas and natural resource wealth enjoyed by Kazakhstan has fuelled massive development in this former capital and led to the rise of a new class of Kazakh, the *novii Kazakh*, who all keep flats in Almaty and return here to party at the weekends.

The development has had its side effects: real estate values have shot through the roof, and it is often as expensive to rent a flat in central Almaty as in London or New York. The knock-on effect of this is that bars, restaurants and shops come and go. High rents mean that many struggle to stay open or are forced to move to new locations and so turnover is high, as are prices.

Development aside, Almaty is an extremely pleasant and laid back town to spend time in. A Tsarist horticulturalist named Edward Baum who lived in Almaty at the end of the nineteenth century inspired a

generation of Almaty's citizens to plant trees, a legacy continued through-out the Soviet peri-od. As a result, when spring arrives, the city comes into bloom almost overnight and walk-ing through its many parks, and along its streets, you sometimes feel you are in a flower-strewn forest rather than a city.

To really appreciate Almaty's stunning setting, take the cable car to Koktubey, a small hill dominated by a TV tower on the city's south-eastern edge. The cable-car terminal is just behind the Palace of the Republic on Dostyk. From the top, you get a magnificent view of the mountains to the south of the city, of the city itself and of the steppe, which stretches endlessly to the north, unbroken until it reaches Siberia.

A word of warning: the mountains in Almaty lie to the south of the city, not the north; this is often confusing when trying to orientate yourself and useful to bear in mind.

SLEEP

1. A-Club Resort
2. Alatau Sanatorium
3. Tau House

EAT

4. Alasha
5. Avlabar
6. Bellagio
7. Dali Restaurant
8. Korea House

Kapchagai

ZHETYSU DISTRICT

13

AREA

ALMALY DISTRICT

2

AREA MAP 2

AUEZOV
DISTRICT

BOSTANDYK
DISTRICT

14

16

7

3 5
Alma Arasan Gorge

0   10   20km

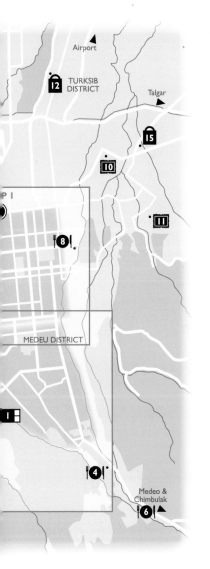

Airport

TURKSIB
DISTRICT

Talgar

MEDEU DISTRICT

Medeo &
Chimbulak

PARTY

9. Most

CULTURE

10. Kazan Cathedral
11. Kensai Graveyard

SHOP

12. Alma-Ata Art Centre
13. Barakholka
14. Camp Bazaar
15. Flea Market
16. Mega Centre Alma-Ata

Central Almaty

The central area of Almaty is the city's historic centre, a monument to Tsarist and Soviet town planning and seemingly unaffected by the massive development which is taking place to the south of the city. Established on a grid system, central Almaty is easy to navigate and a great place to walk thanks to the wide avenues, tree-lined streets and roadside parks, complete with fountains and statues. As you walk you will notice, and occasionally have to negotiate, wide gutters or *aryks*, which divert water from the city's three main rivers for irrigation as well as acting as storm drains in wet weather.

The northern end of central Almaty is dominated by the blue-domed Central Mosque to the east, the bustling Green (Zelony) Bazaar in the centre – perhaps the most Central Asian experience in town and a great place to pop into for a bowl of green tea – and the Arbat or pedestrian street running west of the bazaar along Zhibek Zholy. This name translates as Silk Road and is a destination for street artists, families and a good place to watch the mix of Almaty life.

To the southeast of the Arbat on Kunayev Street is the Arasan Banya, the central public bathhouse. These magnificent baths are the perfect place to relax after a night of hedonism, or perhaps a good place to scrub up before going out.

Right opposite the baths you will find the rectangular Panfilov Park, at the centre of which is the city's main cathedral – a remarkable piece of pastel-coloured wooden architecture from the Tsarist period, reputed to have been built without the use of a single nail.

Running south of the Park on the eastern side of the central area is Dostyk, formerly Lenin Avenue and Almaty's main street, which climbs uphill towards the landmark tower of Hotel Kazakhstan. Walk just beyond the hotel to see the Palace of the Republic, a Soviet building now used mainly for concerts whose golden eaves have a definite feel of the Orient about them.

To the west of Hotel Kazakhstan, along Kurmangazy, you will find the Academy of Sciences – a huge neoclassical edifice with Islamic touches  which was built in the 1950s in the grand Stalinist style, and designed by the famous Moscow architect, Alexey Shchusev.

From the Academy of Sciences, it is well worth strolling down any of the following small streets: Valikhanov, Tulebaev or Baisetov – beautiful in summer or winter and devoid of the traffic of the larger streets which run from north to south. As you walk you will notice plaques on the sides of buildings commemorating well-known figures – artists, writers, politicians and scientists – who lived there during Soviet times.

A walk down Baisetov Street (four streets to the west of the Academy of Sciences) will bring you to the Abai Opera and Ballet Theatre, another highly attractive neo-classical building which, on a good day, with the mountains in the background, is one of Almaty's most iconic sights. If all this walking has exhausted you, pop into L'Affiche, the café facing the Opera House, another of Almaty's gems.

0   5km

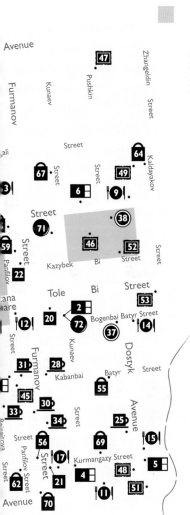

DRINK

18. Boudoir
19. Di Wang
20. Fame
21. La Fete
22. Soho
23. Vitalita

PARTY

35. Bodrum Bar
36. Cacadu Cabaret Bar
37. Cuba
38. Da Freak
39. Esperanza
40. Fashionbar
41. Gas
42. Petroleum
43. Rai
44. Shisha Bar

EAT

8. Boudoir
9. Cooshy Sushi
10. Di Wang
11. Naoro
12. Pomodoro
13. Porto Maltese
14. Safran
15. Thai
16. Zheti Kazyna
17. Zontiki

SLEEP

1. Ambassador Hotel
2. Grand Tien Shan
3. Hotel Alma-Ata
4. Hotel Dostyk
5. Hotel Kazakhstan
6. Hotel Otrar
7. Kazzhol

PLAY

71. Arasan Public Banya
72. Bali Spa Centre

Business District

It may not sound like the natural territory of the hedonist, but the new Business District, home to much of the development taking place in Almaty, is also home to some of the city's main hotels, clubs, cafés and restaurants, so don't judge it on name alone.

The Business District comprises various microdistricts that fall outside the centralized grid pattern of Almaty, making the area seem, at times, confusing. The area is bordered to the east by the Malaya Almatinka (Little Almaty) River and to the west by the Bolshaya Almatinka (Big Almaty) River. These rivers descend from the mountains above the town eventually flowing into Lake Kapchagai and the Ili River in the steppe.

A walk along the banks of the Malaya Almatinka provides a welcome break from city life. Start behind the Arman Cinema on Dostyk and Abai, where the river flows along a concrete channel, but quickly the river returns to its natural environs as the path winds past gnarled trees, large boulders and the flower-filled gardens of Almaty residents.

Alternatively, follow the northern boundary of the Business District, on Abai, one of the city's main axes, and home to the Soviet-built Circus, which looks similar to a giant white spinning top, and the Wedding Palace which, like the circus, was an institution in Soviet society – where else could people get married once all the religious buildings had become museums?

Today it is a tradition following the wedding cermony to make a photographic tour of Almaty's main monuments with your whole wedding entourage, usually in a cavalcade of white limousines bedecked with flowers, horns blaring, and occasionally with a lone video camera operator filming the whole spectacle from the sunroof of the car in front. One of the most popular spots for these nuptial photo shoots is the Monument of Independence in Almaty's Republican Square, a column which competes with Trafalgar Square's Nelson in height, on top of which stands a statue of The Golden Man – a Scythian warrior unearthed just 60km east of Almaty and now a proudly touted symbol of Kazakhstan's rich nomadic ancestry.

On the south-east corner of this square you will find the Central State Museum, an interesting place to update your knowledge of local history, before having lunch at either Vogue Café or Le Jardin on Satpaev. If you naturally gravitate to Vogue, then this end of Satpaev is the place to do some serious shopping for designer clothes – check out Sauvage on the corner of Dostyk and Bureau 1985.

Heading south again and then west on Al-Farabi, you will enter the heart of Almaty's new financial centre – an ambitious project to make Almaty the new regional financial capital. The developers, Capital Partners, who developed the Ritz Carlton in Moscow, have invited world-renowned architects to work on the area's design. By early 2008 the area will be home to the JW Marriott Esentai, which is set to become Almaty's most exclusive address.

Al-Farabi Avenue and the Esentai River (a tributary of the Malaya Almatinka River) mark the southern boundary of the business district. Cross them and you will enter into a world of small wooden houses and orchards, which are vying with the developers for their right to exist.

CULTURE

36. The A. Kastayev State Museum of Art
37. Central State Museum
38. Soros Centre for Contemporary Art

SHOP

39. The A. Kastayev State Museum of Art
40. Aida Kaumenova at the Sadu
41. Ark Gallery
42. Bureau 1985
43. Carpet Shop
44. Central State Museum
45. Concept Store
46. Oyu
47. Ramstore Hypermarket
48. Sauvage Boutique
49. Top Line and Top Secret

PARTY

30. Crystal
31. Euphoria
32. Metro
33. Stars Club
34. Sweet & Spice
35. Tornado

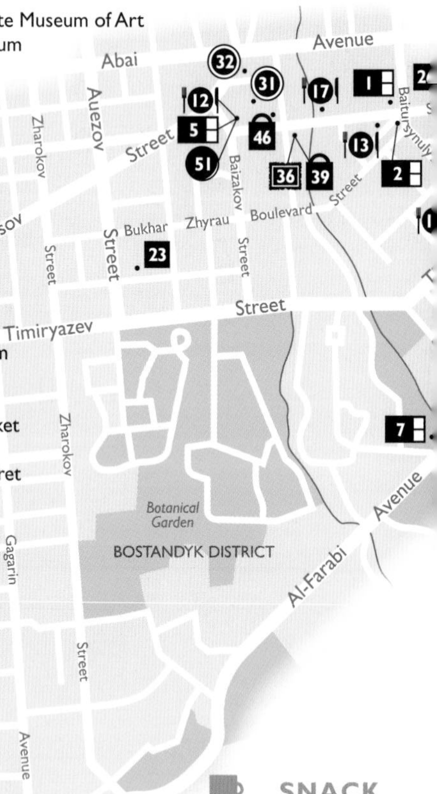

SLEEP

1. Astana International Hotel
2. Grand Aiser Hotel
3. Grand Eurasia Hotel
4. The Holiday Inn
5. Hyatt Regency Almaty
6. InterContinental Almaty
7. JW Marriot Esentai Park

SNACK

28. John's Coffee
29. Le Jardin

PLAY

50. The Ankara Spa
51. Club Olympus Spa & Fitness Centre
52. Luxor Wellness Spa

Abai
Avenue
Auezov Street
Zharokov
Zhandosov Street
Bukhar Zhyrau
Baizakov Boulevard
Timiryazev
Street
Rozybakiev
Gagarin
Street
Zharokov
Botanical Garden
BOSTANDYK DISTRICT
Al-Farabi
Avenue
Baitursynuly
Street

Business District local map

0   5km   10km

sleep...

The true hedonist never sleeps, partying until dawn, but for the weary Almaty has a comprehensive selection of hotels – although you'll find the majority of are geared towards the businessman, not the tourist, with prices to match: cheap or boutique hotels do not exist here.

The good news, however, is that the arrival of two brand new luxury hotels (the JW Marriott Esentai Park and the Holiday Inn), with more in the pipeline, is revolutionizing the quality of accommodation in Almaty, sending the established hotels into a frenzy of reconstruction, renovation and refurbishment (three words best summed up by the catch-all Russian word *remont*).

At the top end, the international chains – the Hyatt and the Intercontinental – offer a reliable international standard of service, a concept which should be treated like gold dust in a region where service can often come in a sullen, unresponsive package. These two hotels are situated in the Business District, along with a number of other hotels such as the Grand Aiser, the Grand Eurasia Hotel and the Astana International – cheaper than the international chains, and Turkish-run, so adhering to a higher standard than regular hotels.

Tucked away in Almaty's central district, the newly opened Grand Tien Shan Hotel and the Ambassador and Dostyk Hotels, which have both been recently renovated, are perfectly situated if you want to explore the centre of the city by foot. Beware, however, that new does not necessarily mean that everything is in good working order. If you are prepared for the occasional malfunction, you will find yourself far better able to relax than if you come expecting the best of western style service and standards.

Perhaps Almaty's most beloved hotel is the Hotel Kazakhstan (right), which dominates the city skyline and even turns up on the back of the 5,000 tenge note. Recent renovations have perked up what was a fairly standard Soviet offering, and like many of the hotel rooms in the city, especially in the business district, the upper floor rooms offer fabulous views of the mountains to the south.

Two other ex-Soviet hotels are the Hotel Otrar adjoining Panfilov Park and the Hotel Alma-Ata opposite the Abai Opera and Ballet Theatre. You can't beat their locations, and they are institutions that are worth seeing, especially if you are nostalgic for a bit of the old USSR.

If you are looking for peace, quiet and fresh air, we can recommend the ex-Soviet Alatau Sanatorium. Although it sounds menacing, this was the Communist

Party elite's venue of choice for R&R in Soviet times. Situated roughly 15km west of the city centre, it can take a considerable amount of time to get there if the traffic is heavy, and so is worth visiting only if you have the time to relax and enjoy one of the most unspoilt views of the Zhailiskii Alatau Mountains Almaty has to offer.

Prices in the guide range from the price of a standard single room to the price of the presidential suite (if there is one). Because Almaty is a year-round destination, there is no official high or low season.

A-Club Resort, Al-Farabi, Remizovka Gorge
Tel: 271 7484   www.a-club.kz
Rates: 11,000–127,000 tenge

Situated just three minutes from the centre of the city, the A-Club Resort's 60 rooms are a great place to stay if you want to be outside town, but with quick and easy access, should you need it. The hotel is located one kilometre south of Al Farabi and the Business District and has clean rooms each

with its own balcony and, more importantly, fresh air, which is palpable as soon as you arrive. The A-Club benefits from a neighbouring spa, which guests can use at half price – a very reasonable 2,000 tenge for the day. Facilities include a 25-metre swimming pool, a Finnish and Turkish sauna, and the use of a gym.

Style 6, Atmosphere 7, Location 8

Alatau Sanatorium, Upper Kamenka Village
Tel: 254 9765
Rates: 16,900–32,400 tenge

Originally established during Soviet times as a place of rest and relaxation for the Communist Party elite, Alatau Sanatorium, or 'health resort' as it prefers to be known, is now open to all. Set in a large area of wooded grounds roughly 15km to the west of the city centre, the sanatorium offers fresh air and quiet, a spectacular view of the Zhailiskii Alatau mountains, and – should you be interested – an intriguing range of health treatments. Inside,

the décor has barely changed since the apparatchiks moved out, so this gives a fascinating insight into the grand old days of the Soviet Union. With the 18-hole Nurtau Golf Club in the grounds, an aqua park attached to the hotel, mineral water treatments and billiards, paintball, a gym, kiosk, souvenir shop and even a post office, you almost don't need to go into town, but if you do, bear in mind it can take time in the traffic.

Style 7, Atmosphere 7, Location 8

Ambassador Hotel, 121 Zheltoksan St (Karasai Batyr), Almaly

Tel: 250 8989 or 244 7373 www.ambassadorhotel.kz
Rates: 26,500–52,000 tenge

Originally constructed in 1936, the Ambassador Hotel calls itself the first

boutique hotel in Kazakhstan. While not necessarily our definition of a boutique hotel, the Ambassador has a certain charm that makes it more unique and a favourite of ours, especially given the central location. Turkish-run and popular among the predominately Turkish clientele, most of the Ambassador's 55 rooms open onto a balcony – the nicest of which are on the hotel's rear overlooking a quiet courtyard. The rooms are surprisingly spacious for the building's age, and the more expensive ones come with a Jacuzzi. Saltanat, the Ambassador's Turkish restaurant, is open 24 hours a day, and the two outside terraces are always full of lively Turkish businessmen chatting the night away and especially busy whenever Galatasaray is playing. Don't miss Bodrum Bar (see Party) in the Ambassador's lower level where the live Turkish music (and crowd) gets livelier as the night goes on.

Style 8, Atmosphere 8, Location 8

Astana International Hotel, 113 Baitursynuly St, Bostandyk

Tel: 250 7050 www.astana-hotel.com
Rates: 22,500–34,500 tenge

In a good position for the new financial district, the four-star Astana International is popular with businessmen and tourists alike. Currently undergoing reconstruction in parts, this ex-Soviet hotel is slowly becoming more and more attractive. Rooms have a view of the mountains or the steppe and some have balconies (make sure to ask if you want one). All standard rooms come with a shower, tea and coffee facilities (a nice touch) and have paid WiFi access. Run by the same Turkish management company as the Ambassador Hotel in Central Almaty, the service is friendly and

efficient. Located just over the road from the Indian restaurant Namaste and not far from John's Coffee and nightclub Crystal, you barely have to leave the hotel to have a good time. Oh, and the Hotel Astana offers a free transfer to the hotel from the airport.

Style 6, Atmosphere 6, Location 8

Grand Aiser Hotel, Satpaev St (Baitursynuly), Bostandyk
Tel: 250 3350   www.grandaiserhotel.kz
Rates: 15,000–45,000 tenge

Located opposite the Astana International Hotel in the Business District, the Grand Aiser offers a good, economical alternative to business travellers who might not want to spend the kind of cash required at the Hyatt Regency

just down the street on Satpaev. This hotel is Turkish-run by a company that operates a number of other hotels in the city, including the Grand Eurasia Hotel (see page 26). While not necessarily boutique in style, the Grand Aiser provides a cheap and cheerful option in a hotel market dominated by high-end business travel. That said the Grand Aiser has a variety of clean and spacious rooms ranging from singles to junior suites and even apartments for longer-term stays. The apartments are kitted up with replica Baroque antiques, an en-suite bathroom with Jacuzzi, a dining table for eight, and the final touch – faux leather upholstered furniture in the sitting room.

Style 6, Atmosphere 6, Location 8

Grand Eurasia Hotel, 19a Zholdasbekov Street (Dostyk), Samal

Tel: 264 8113 or 262 2693
Rates: 15,000–75,000 tenge

Operated by the same company as the Grand Aiser Hotel (see page 25), the Grand Eurasia Hotel offers very similar accommodation and amenities, albeit slightly updated. Located in the middle of the Samal district, one of

the first areas businesses moved to prior to heading out along Al-Farabi as they do now. The Grand Eurasia is well positioned with easy access to Dostyk for a quick getaway into the mountains or conversely to the many bars and restaurants nearer the city centre. The Grand Eurasia suites offer more luxury than that seen in the standard rooms and come with their own espresso maker alongside ornate reproduction furniture. There's also a sauna and Turkish restaurant serving up authentic *dolma* and *mezzes*. Given its central location, the Grand Eurasia provides a convenient jumping-off point for exploring what Almaty has to offer.

Style 6, Atmosphere 6, Location 8

Grand Tien Shan Hotel, 115 Bogenbai Batyr (Kunaev), Medeu

Tel: 244 9600   www.ts-hotels.kz
Rates: 26,000–136,000 tenge

Opened in 2006, the Grand Tien Shan Hotel sits in the neo-classically designed building of what used to be Kazakhstan's Ministry of Geology. With its wonderfully central location, just opposite Kunaev Park, this is the perfect starting point for a walking tour of the city. Inside, the hotel combines

stately elegance and lavishly decorated rooms to create a sense of style and sophistication. Be sure to request a room on the park-side, and be woken by the marvellous mountain views from which the hotel takes its name. Not to be missed is a visit to the Bali Spa Centre (see Play) in the hotel's lower level and home to the best Balinese massage in Almaty. Although a note of warning – the hotel looks polished on the surface (and while we still highly recommend it), there have been reports that the local management style doesn't quite hold up to European standards of service.

Style 7, Atmosphere 8, Location 8

The Holiday Inn, 10 Timiryazeva Street, Bostandyk
Tel: n/a
Rates: 38,000–41,000 tenge

With the opening planned for November 2007, The Holiday Inn will be Almaty's first international four-star hotel. Situated a stone's throw from its five-star sister, the Intercontinental Ankara Hotel, The Holiday Inn offers a more affordable, less luxurious destination for business travellers and tourists. Each of its 230 rooms will have baths and the majority will have a mountain view. The bright and airy restaurant on the ground floor will offer international cuisine with some local favourites. With prices around the 40,000 tenge mark, The Holiday Inn will offer good value for money.

Style 8, Atmosphere 7, Location 7

Hotel Alma-Ata, 85 Kabanbai Batyr (corner of Panfilov), Almaly
Tel: 272 0070 www.hotel-alma-ata.com
Rates: 15,000–32,000 tenge

The Alma-Ata, built in 1967, was one of Almaty's first grand hotels, and stands as a monument to the Soviet architecture of the era. Located in the heart of Central Almaty, Hotel Alma-Ata is a prime spot from which to explore the city's parks, cafés and restaurants. While renovation to the sixth, seventh and eighth floors in early 2007 provided a much needed update, the rooms remain plain and simple. However, all the mod cons of a five-star hotel cannot compare to the Alma-Ata's mountain views. Request a room

facing the mountains, wake at sunrise, and Almaty's picture-perfect panorama (pre-midday smog) will unveil itself before your groggy eyes. Before checking-out, let the lobby piano and violin duet serenade you while taking in the black and white photographs of 1960s Almaty that line the walls of Retro restaurant to see what the city looked like before the building boom came to town.

Style 6, Atmosphere 8, Location 9

Hotel Dostyk, 36 Kurmangazy St (Kunaev), Medeu
Tel: 258 2270
Rates: 47,500–250,000 tenge

Built in the early 1980s as part of the then First Secretary of the Communist Party's plan to aggrandize Almaty, the Dostyk Hotel was the hotel of choice for the Communist Party elite. In fact, the tradition continued after Independence as President Nazarbayev's 60th birthday party was

held here too. Having recently undergone complete renovation, this five-storey hotel now offers a spa, sauna, fitness centre, gym, swimming pool, hamam and Jacuzzi. The hotel boasts a great location in the centre of downtown Almaty, not far from the Academy of Sciences and the cafés Biskvit and CoffeeDelia and is very popular with businessmen.

Style 8, Atmosphere 7, Location 8

Hotel Kazakhstan, 52 Dostyk Avenue, (Kurmangazy), Medeu

Tel: 259 0909 or 291 9101 www.hotel-kazakhstan.kz
Rates: 16,000–48,000 tenge

Perhaps one of Almaty's, if not Kazakhstan's, most well-known buildings is the Hotel Kazakhstan. Constructed in the early 1970s under Kunaev's leadership (Kazakhstan's former First Secretary who redeveloped Dostyk to become an avenue of skyscrapers), the hotel itself stretches more than 100-

metres high, and can be seen from most vantage points in the city. At night, its golden crown shines bright, and the digits '2030' are illuminated on its side – no, not indicating the time, but rather the President's goal for when Kazakhstan will reach the pinnacle of its success. In 2006, gradual renovations started and are still under way, so when booking a room, be sure to request one that has been renovated (and with a mountain vista) – unless you want to discover the less glamorous style of Soviet accommodation. Hotel Kazakhstan's crowning glory is Cosmos, its 26th floor restaurant that provides an unimpeded panorama of the city's snow-capped peaks – well worth a visit even if you're not a hotel guest.

Style 7, Atmosphere 7, Location 9

Hotel Otrar, 73 Gogol Street (Kunaev), Medeu
Tel: 250 6806
Rates: 16,000–93,000 tenge

Built in 1981 and a firm favourite in the late Soviet period, the 161-room Hotel Otrar has barely changed since, with *dezhurnayas* still overseeing the business of individual floors. However, the hotel's enviable 'downtown' location right next to Panfilov Park merits, we feel, its inclusion. Book a front-facing room on the fourth or fifth floor and you'll be rewarded with a

view over the tree tops and the domes of Zenkov Cathedral towards the Zhailiskii Alatau mountains to the south. The vast yurt-shaped restaurant with scenes from Kazakh folklore painted in miniaturist style on the ceiling makes breakfast a meal to be savoured, and the adjoining Otrar Travel Company make planning days out of Almaty painfree.

Style 6, Atmosphere 6, Location 7

Hyatt Regency Almaty, 29/6 Satpaev, Bostandyk
Tel: 250 1234
Rates: 54,000–300,000 tenge

The fact that this was the first five-star hotel to be built in Almaty is telling

from the outside, but once inside, Hyatt hospitality kicks in. The Regency Club on the 10th floor offers personalized services to guests staying on the top two floors, while the Olympus Health Club is considered by many to be one of the best health clubs in town. Rooms offer a queen-sized bed, armchair, balcony and views of the mountains as standard and the customer service throughout the hotel is exemplary. The 24 hour yurt café in the main lobby injects a touch of Central Asia into the international surroundings and also serves one of the best lattes in town, which may account for its popularity as a meeting-place. If taking a taxi, it is useful to ask for the hotel by its former name, the 'Rahat Palace'.

Style 8, Atmosphere 9, Location 7

InterContinental Almaty, The Ankara in Kazakhstan, 181 Zholtoksan Street (Timiryazev), Bostandyk
Tel: 250 5000   www.intercontinental.com
Rates: 60,000–500,000 tenge

The InterContinental Almaty (formerly the Regent Almaty) has renovated its 290 rooms to include nine executive and two presidential suites plus three Club InterContinental floors and a 24-hour Club Lounge. A five-star busi-

ness hotel with a convenient location in the Business District and walking distance to central Almaty, the InterContinental Almaty (often referred to as the Ankara) offers its guests a Newspaper Direct service, which delivers over 500 newspapers from around the world. In addition to all mod cons, the InterContinental Almaty has a delectable array of dining experiences including the top floor Belvedere Grill Room, which offers stunning views of the Tien Shan Mountains, the Bosphorus Turkish restaurant (see Eat), and the Member's Bar where live jazz provides nightly entertainment. If it's R&R you're after, pay a visit to the Ankara Spa for a massage or body treatment, and then order from the hotel's special Pillow Menu for a deep night's sleep.

Style 8, Atmosphere 8, Location 9

JW Marriott Hotel at Esentai Park, Al-Farabi Avenue and the Esentai River, Bostandyk
Tel: n/a www.esentai.com
Rates: n/a

Soon to be Almaty's most prestigious address, the JW Marriott Hotel at Esentai Park will open in early 2008, and will create a new urban centre for the Business District. Esentai Park, a project by Capital Partners, the Almaty-based development firm that has been recreating the city's skyline with

world-class projects such as the new Almaty Financial Centre, will be a mixed-use complex comprising the JW Marriott hotel, office space, residential buildings and a shopping and entertainment centre. Designed by renowned architects Skidmore, Owings & Merrill, the 162-metre Esentai Tower will become Almaty's tallest building. The five-star hotel will have 175 rooms and 47 serviced apartments, and is set to become the new benchmark of luxury in Kazakhstan. The shopping and entertainment complex will open slightly later, and will have a movie theatre, a spa and fitness centre with tennis courts and swimming pool, and high-end retailers including the French bakery Paul and Hediard, the gourmet Parisian market and restaurant.

Style n/a, Atmosphere n/a, Location n/a

Kazzhol, 127/1 Gogol, Almaly
Tel: 250 8944 www.kazju.kz
Rates: 9,300–26,000 tenge

As a three-star hotel, what Kazzhol lacks in luxury it makes up for with its quiet, hidden location in a courtyard between Gogol and Zhibek Zholy and Nauryzbai Batyr and Seifullin. Kazzhol is clean and tidy, with efficient service and, for Almaty, cheap. This six-floor hotel is popular with the non-business crowd, NGOs and backpackers, and its 119 rooms, although small at the

cheaper end, contain all mod cons. Situated to the north of the city, it is easy to reach Tsum and the Arbat on foot from here. If you are feeling stretched by extravagance in Almaty's bars and restaurants, Kazzhol could be the place for you.

Style 6, Atmosphere 6, Location 7

Tau House, Tau Dastarkhan Family Resort, Ile Alatau National Park, Alma Arasan Gorge
Tel: 270 5729 or 275 9140 www.tauhouse.kz
Rates: 22,000–85,000 tenge

Tau House is part of the Dastarkhan Complex on the road up to Alma Arasan and Big Almaty Lake. Situated around a central landscaped courtyard full of trees and shrubs, entrance to your room is gained via the front door

of a series of small chalets, each of which gives access to just two hotel rooms (unless you are splashing out and taking a Diplomat's suite). This semi-private access makes the hotel rooms more apartment-like than a hotel, and combined with the fresh mountain air and open balconies with panoramic views of the mountains, Tau House makes a great alternative to the traffic-filled city below, but be prepared to travel a little bit. Don't let this deter you though; the great thing about the Dastarkhan Complex is that you have six restaurants on your doorstep, including the renowned Georgian restaurant, Avlabar, and you can also take advantage of a wide range of sporting facilities including tennis, volleyball and the neighbouring spa centre.

Style 8, Atmosphere 8, Location 7

eat...

Traditional Kazakh cuisine is composed of mutton- and pasta-based dishes such as *besparmak*, which translates as five fingers and refers to the way the dish was traditionally eaten. For the hedonist's version, head to Zheti Kazyna, the best local restaurant in town, which will serve up a surprisingly delicious home-made *besparmak* (with a knife and fork) in an elaborately decorated Khan's yurt. Finish the meal with a quart of *kumiss* (fermented mare's milk) or *shubat* (fermented camel's milk) for a truly authentic touch.

The traditional penchant for meat and pasta could explain why Italian food is so popular in Almaty. You will find Italian dishes on just about half of all menus, although the best Italian can be found at the VIP haunt Borgo Antico, or for a more homely version, at Pomodoro. In fact, the popularity of Italian food has led to fights at dawn in the local market when kitchen porters try to buy up supplies of rocket (*arugula*) for their salads.

A desire to satisfy everybody often results in lengthy menus that go as far as listing the types of cigarettes and chewing gum the restaurant has on offer. It's not infrequent that having chosen something on one of these biblically long menus, you'll find that the restaurant doesn't have what you want. A short menu, we have concluded, is a promising sign, boding well for both the restaurant and the food. Most restaurants have a menu in English, and if they don't we will warn you. Waiters, on the other hand, tend to speak limited English, although there is usually somebody who can translate.

Almaty offers a wide selection of cuisines for the discerning customer. Our favourite is the Thai restaurant on Dostyk, which has served up faultless Thai food since 2002. Asian Wok, further up Dostyk, produces delicious Indian and Chinese food; Cooshi Sushi, one of dozens of restaurants offering sushi, is another favourite; while Boudouir, newly opened on Bogenbai Batyr, presents exciting global fusion cuisine; and Porto Maltese on Panfilov offers up delicious fresh fish from Norway, Italy, Serbia and Dubai. Unless you want to revert to meat and pasta, food miles are best not discussed.

Don't be surprised either if you find a fellow customer yelling '*devushka*' or '*molodoi chelovyek*' at the top of his voice. This customary way of getting the waitress/waiter's attention can seem a bit harsh, but you will soon learn that it is the best way to get served, and not considered offensive at all. Service in restaurants

varies: some restaurants such as Thai, Borgo Antico, Bosphorus, The Grill Restaurant, Bellagio, Cooshy Sushi and Sadu have faultless and very attentive service; at others, it may be hard to get the waiters' attention and food can take a long time to be served. Occasionally service may even seem petulant. This is partly to do with supply and demand: the large number of restaurants and bars opening cannot keep up with the supply of good waiters, and partly to do with management styles, which are slowly emerging from the Soviet chrysalis.

Many restaurants offer a business lunch – a set menu at a set price or at a discount (usually of about 20% off normal prices) – and from May to September the vast majority of restaurants spill out onto the adjoining pavement, their bustling terraces becoming a great place to relax on a summer's evening. We have based prices on what it costs for one person to eat two courses with a glass or two of wine. Bon appetit!

Alasha, 20 Ospanov Street, Medeu

Tel: 271 5670 or 271 5671 www.alasha.kz
Open: daily, noon–midnight   8,000 tenge
Central Asian

Tucked in a side street off Dostyk Avenue on the way towards the mountains, you could be forgiven for thinking that you had come across a tiled mud brick mosque at the entrance to Alasha. Set around a courtyard, Alasha provides a truly Central Asian experience. In the summer guests recline on

tapchans (raised Central Asian platforms) or dine in one of the private rooms overlooking the courtyard. In the main hall the mud brick walls, painted ceiling, open kitchen with tandoor oven and Uzbek textiles and pots combine to give the feeling of being right in the heart of traditional Uzbekistan. The food – mainly Uzbek with some Kazakh thrown in for good measure – is tasty and the service is friendly, with the waiters dressed as young Uzbek boys in *tipiteca* hats and striped *caftan* shirts. If you want to eat somewhere quiet, then Alasha is not for you: at 9pm the show starts with ear splittingly loud music, dancers and acrobats. If you're in the mood to have fun though – the experience is definitely worth it.

Food 7, Service 7, Atmosphere 7/8

Asian Wok, 248 Dostyk Avenue (Kazhymukan), Medeu

Tel: 264 4812
Open: daily, noon–11pm   9,000 tenge
Chinese/Indian

With the opening of Asian Wok in summer 2007, Executive Chef Bappi Sharma, who has spent years perfecting his flavours in Moscow, introduced a new standard of Chinese and Indian cooking to Almaty's culinary scene.

Bappi designed the menu and concocted three sauces that inspire a unique blend of fusion and flavours; his ginger and spring onion sauce, black bean sauce and hot Szechuan bean sauce are not to be missed and can be sampled atop a variety of fresh seafood and meats. The Indian menu is equally as delectable with classic *biryanis* next to tandoor-cooked fish and prawn *tikkas* marinated in Indian spices and herbs. The most difficult part of Asian Wok, therefore, comes in deciding between the fragrant flavours. If that's the case, seek guidance from Bappi; he's happy to assist and may even create something special for you on the spot – it's that kind of personal attention that makes Asian Wok a favourite.

Food 9, Service 9, Atmosphere 7

Avlabar, Tau Dastarkhan, Tau Dastarkhan Family Resort, Ile Alatau National Park, Alma Arasan Gorge

Tel: 270 5729 www.tau-dastarkhan.kz
Open: daily, 11am–2am   7,000 tenge
Georgian

Named after an Armenian district in Tiblisi, Avlabar is known for its true Georgian hospitality. Located at Tau Dastarkhan in the Alma Arasan Valley, Avlabar is one of six restaurants in this complex that sits in the foothills of the Zhailiskii Alatau Mountains. Situated around a large pond, the restau-

rants have spacious outdoor cafés connected by walking paths, making it
easy to amble through each until one provokes your taste buds. The culinary
offerings include Kazakh, Japanese, Soviet-style, and a traditional hunting-
lodge, but it's the wholesome flavours of Avlabar's Georgian kitchen that has
people from Almaty raving. Avlabar offers all the traditional classics – from
fresh *khachapuri* (cheese-filled flat bread) to *lobio* (kidney bean salad) and
pkhali (beets in a garlic and walnut sauce) and meat and fish dishes cooked
in delicious sauces like *tkemali* (tart plum) and *bazha* (walnut with pomegranate). Finally, no Georgian meal is complete without a few toasts, so try a
bottle (or two) of Georgian wine; Mukuzani or Tsinandali are guaranteed
not to disappoint.

Food 8, Service 7, Atmosphere 7

Bellagio, 197 Gornaya Street, Road to Medeo
Tel: 250 2409
Open: daily, noon–midnight   12,000 tenge
Italian

Bellagio has a reputation as a restaurant for presidents. Not only is it
reportedly President Nazarbayev's favourite spot in Almaty, but it has also
entertained the likes of Vladimir Putin and Bill Clinton. Located on Gornaya
(the extension of Dostyk Avenue that runs all the way up to the mountains), Bellagio is the poshest of all the Gornaya riverside restaurants, and is
situated just before the gates that go through to the Ili-Alatau National Park
on the way to Medeo and Chimbulak. It offers one of the quickest escapes
from the bustle of the city; during the summer, the outside terrace is com-

plemented by the sound of the Malaya Almatinka River rushing down the mountainside. Bellagio claims to have introduced the first exclusive Italian menu to Almaty and attracts the city's most elite clientele who come to dine on its fresh selection of seafood. Given its popularity for private functions, it is advisable to ring in advance for reservations.

Food 7, Service 8, Atmosphere 8

Bibliotheque, 116 Dostyk Avenue (Satpaev), Medeu
Tel: 262 6122
Open: daily, noon–midnight   6,500 tenge
European

From the outside Bibliotheque's entrance is carved with famous quotes about wine, our favourite being Alexandre Dumas' wise observation that 'wine…is the intellectual part of the meal'. Inside, books line the walls in well-spaced shelves while tea leaves and all their accoutrements are stashed away neatly in their own mounted niche. Bibliotheque has been a favourite among the VIP clientele who have dined here since its opening in 2003, perhaps because of the understated charm that creates a sense of being at home amongst one's closest friends. Classical music is paired with classic European cuisine and impressionist paintings decorate the walls. The elegant place settings, piano, eclectic chandeliers, fireplace and classics lined up on the shelves, like Omar Khayam poetry, *Don Quixote* and *The Alchemist*, are the details that are sure to make dining at Bibliotheque a truly memorable evening.

Food 8, Service 8, Atmosphere 7

Borgo Antico, 11/6 Iskendirov Street, Gorni Gigant

Tel: 293 5151 www.borgoantico.kz
Open: daily, noon–midnight   8,000 tenge
Italian

Not since Marco Polo travelled the Silk Road over 700 years ago has Central Asia seen such a fine Italian. Yet Borgo Antico's vaulted red brick ceilings, warm tiles and rustic Tuscan feel are situated in a quiet residential area, and has quickly become the haunt of the Almaty elite. Take a bite of their prawn and rocket salad steeped in balsamic vinegar, and you can see why. The a la carte menu offers a wide selection of mouth-watering dishes.

Try the small penne pasta with fresh salmon – flown in twice weekly from Dubai with sea bass, lobster, red snapper and calamari added to the haul. These fresh fish dishes are a perfect complement to the more traditional main courses like *osso bucco* and *risotto*. Trained by a much-loved Italian director, who sadly passed away, the waiters are able to recommend and decant the most suitable wine from the restaurant's extensive cellar to complement your meal, and they work as a team to ensure that you, as the customer, are never left wanting.

Food 7, Service 9, Atmosphere 8

Bosphorus, InterContinental Hotel, 181 Zheltoksan St (Timiryazev), Bostandyk
Tel: 250 5000
Open: 7–11pm. Closed Sundays.   5,500 tenge
Turkish

With pictures of Ortakoy Mosque, the Sweet Waters of Istanbul and other Turkish delights on the walls, Bosphorus is a home away from home for

some of the many Turkish expats living in Almaty. Serving Turkish and Ottoman dishes, you only have to try their mouthwatering selection of *mezzes*, which arrive on a tray for you to choose from, to see why. Situated on the second floor of the InterContintental Hotel, the early evening views of the mountains from the summer terrace are unsurpassable. As befits a restaurant in a five-star hotel, the service is impeccable – some of the best in town – and the restaurant is so willing to please that they will even provide low calorie or low salt meals on request, plus the meat is halal and Bosphorus even caters for Ramadan with an Iftar buffet to break your fast.

Food 8, Service 9, Atmosphere 7

Boudoir, 134 Bogenbai Batyr (Ablai Khan), Almaly

Tel: 272 5555
Open: daily, noon–2am
Eclectic/Fusion

The only place in Almaty where you can eat live mud crab from the creeks of Australia, Boudoir takes global fusion cuisine to the extreme. Ozzy chef Shane Brierly and his Thai wife come hot from Lotus One in Dubai and can create almost anything you can imagine, and more. From foie gras crostini to

fillet of Australian crocodile with ancho-chilli, green beans and coconut and home-made ice cream to die for, this is a truly decadent experience. If nothing on the ample menu takes your fancy, Shane and his wife are happy to experiment. The cocktails, mixed by a London mixologist and using local ingredients (such as Almaty apples), are out of this world. Set in a sleek, dark, wood-panelled interior lit by candles, this stylish venue will appeal to the hedonist in all of you.

Food 9, Service 8, Atmosphere 7

Cooshy Sushi, 41/15 Gogol St (Zenkov), Medeu

Tel: 273 8462 or 273 5198
Open: daily, noon–midnight   3,500 tenge
Japanese/Sushi

Sushi is not an obvious choice in the largest land-locked country in the world, but it's all the rage in Almaty. Opened in summer 2007, Cooshy Sushi is Almaty's first *kaiten* sushi bar, serving fresh *nigiri*, *maki* and *temaki* from a

conveyer belt that winds its way through the restaurant's loft-style interior, with its exposed brick walls and industrial design accents making it one of the hippest spots in town. Prepared by Japanese chefs (a rare commodity in most of Almaty's sushi establishments), the sushi is served on colour-coded plates with each colour denoting its cost. Simply grab your favourite *sashimi* or *tataki* as it passes by you, and when you're done, the bill is tallied by counting the coloured plates. Popular for both lunch and dinner, a full menu of Japanese-prepared meals is also available. Don't miss the *teppanyaki* room downstairs, a popular spot for business lunches and meetings, where the chefs work their culinary magic right in front of you.

Food 8, Service 8, Atmosphere 8

Dali Restaurant, Zhailjau Golf Resort, Kargaly
Tel: 277 7621   www.zgr.kz
Open: daily, 10am–midnight daily   11,000 tenge
Mediterranean

A golf course might be one of the last places you would expect Salvador Dali to turn up, but Zhailjau Golf Resort (see Play) not only has his artwork on display but also an entire restaurant devoted to the Surrealist painter. Dali's, located inside the Zhailjau clubhouse, has its walls flanked with the artist's masterpieces as well as the pièce de résistance – a giant, ceiling-sized reproduction of one of Dali's famous Melting Clocks. No one knows 'why Dali?', but we can only guess it's a subtle reminder that when on the greens or sampling some of the mouth-watering Mediterranean cuisine Dali's chefs serve up, one doesn't need to be reminded of the rigidity of time. Time is relative, as Dali believed, and enjoying another glass of chilled wine while gazing out at,

quite possibly, the most pristine view of the Tien Shan Mountains that Almaty has to offer, is the perfect way to spend an afternoon.

Food 7, Service 7, Atmosphere 8

Di Wang, 75 Zhambyl St (Tchaikovskovo), Almaly
Tel: 272 3810 www.diwang.kz
Open: daily, noon–midnight   6,500 tenge
Chinese/Japanese

Tucked away on a quiet side street, Di Wang houses one of Almaty's most popular scenes. Both a restaurant and lounge bar (see Drink), Di Wang is always packed with a devoted clientele. Designed by the leading designer of

the French modern furniture company Ligne Roset, Di Wang's has an unique interior in the city. Images of Chinese and Japanese emperors grace the wall while oak wood floors, white leather chairs and a glass aquarium full of exotic fish complement the natural colours and minimalist Asian décor. Singaporean chefs dish up some of the tastiest Japanese and Chinese cuisine in Almaty with house specialities including Peking Duck and Shark Fin Soup. There's also a full sushi menu, a good value business lunch and a dim sum menu, which could be the brunch-time cure after a long night of partying; pair it with a traditional tea ceremony and you'll be on the road to recovery.

Food 7, Service 8, Atmosphere 8

The Grill Restaurant, Hyatt Regency Hotel, 29/6 Satpaev St, Bostandyk

Tel: 250 2663
Open: daily, noon–3pm and 6pm–midnight   12,500 tenge
Steakhouse

Expensive, but if you are looking for the best steak in town, this is the place. Situated on the ground floor of the Hyatt Regency Hotel, this bistro style restaurant with wood-panelled walls offers prime Black Angus steaks, T-bone

steaks, strip loin, tenderloin, rib eye and, if you prefer, lamb, pork and seafood (tuna, salmon, monkfish, halibut, prawns) – any of which can be sizzled on the grill. Plus, there is always one type of steak on the menu for the business lunch served between noon and 3pm, which comes in at a much more modest price. The service, as befits a restaurant in a top-class hotel, is efficient and understated, and there is even a non-smoking section, something of a rarity in Kazakhstan. So if you are craving a good old-fashioned steak, head on in.

Food 8, Service 8, Atmosphere 7

Korea House, 2 Gogol Street, Medeu
Tel: 293 9687 or 293 9692
Open: daily, noon–midnight   5,500 tenge
Korean

The prevalence of Korean restaurants in Almaty and Central Asia in general dates back to 1937 when Stalin moved over 200,000 Korean settlers living in Russia's Far East to Central Asia to prevent them, ostensibly, from spying for Japan. Now over double that number of Koreans live in the region, and ladies selling Korean salads are an everyday part of life in Central Asian

bazaars. Korea House, just 50 metres from the entrance to Gorky Park on Gogol Street, is undoubtedly the smartest Korean restaurant, attracting a top-class clientele. Fresh and light with lots of greenery and bamboo placemats on the dark Asian-style furniture, Korea House is renowned for its 'Korean-style' service, with waiters bowing to their guests and always serving guests with two hands to show respect. The chef comes from South Korea and creates deliciously spicy food.

Food 7, Service 8, Amosphere 8

Namaste, Baitursynov St (Satpaev), Bostandyk

Tel: 292 2484

Open: daily, 11am–midnight   3,000 tenge

Indian

If you're looking for homely Indian food, look no further – Namaste is the answer. Conveniently located for the Hyatt, Aiser and Astana International Hotels, Namaste is an Indian restaurant that, if judged by décor alone, couldn't be mistaken for anything else. Popular with the foreign crowd, the Thai-

trained Indian chef's specialities include flavoured naan breads, tandoor dishes cooked in a clay oven and an infinite variety of delicious vegetarian dishes. Accompanied by Indian music videos and Bollywood movies this is an informal, but spicy, dining experience.

Food 8, Service 8, Atmosphere 7

Naoro, 17 Abai Avenue (Pushkin), Medeu

Tel: 291 1145

Open: 7–11pm Tues–Sat   13,000 tenge

International Fusion

Klimt's Judith from his 'golden phase' adorns the wall of Almaty's chicest new restaurant Naoro, meaning 'On Gold' (Na from Russian and Oro from Italian). So lavish is the menu that gold leaf even turns up on some of its dishes. Chef Julian Sperondio worked with the legendary Pierre Gagnaire, one of the leaders in the fusion cuisine movement, and he does his mentor justice here. With director Sam Sedecias (formerly of Nobu London) he has created a simple formula concentrating on a main ingredient, a complementary garnish and exotic sauces; try the lamb with coffee chickpea puree, bok choy and cardamom sauce. Unlike many local restaurants, Sedecias has

 shunned the VIP room approach with the introduction of the 'Chocolate' room – Almaty's first communal dining experience. Where better to try Naoro's Valhrona chocolate fondue with a glass of Remy Martin's Louis XIII cognac. Reservations are essential, but pop in for a cocktail and some tapas-style canapes while waiting for your table.

Food 9, Service 9, Atmosphere 9

Piano Bar Mardi Gras, Palladium Restaurant Complex, 275 Furmanov Street (Al-Farabi), Medeu

Tel: 260 8900 www.palladium.kz
Open: noon–3pm Monday–Friday   2,000 tenge
International

The star of the show at Palladium's Piano Bar Mardi Gras is Kazakhstan's one and only transparent Schimmel grand piano. The piano's striking appearance lends an air of elegance and style to this restaurant, which is located in the heart of the Business District. The Piano Bar is a favourite lunch spot for the embassy employees, top managers and international companies that have offices nearby. Only opened to the public for lunch, the German chefs cook up plenty of reasons to schedule a meeting (or two) here. An extensive wine list, plus a full bar and a first-rate selection of cigars, suggests you

might schedule a light afternoon post-Piano Bar. The other venues at Palladium include Cotton Restaurant and Be Bop Disco which, along with Piano Bar, are available for hire for private functions, so when you need to entertain your nearest and dearest, go on and take the entire complex for a night of true hedonism.

Food 7, Service 7, Atmosphere 7

Pomodoro, 108 Panfilov St (Bogenbai), Almaly
Tel: 261 8326
Open: noon–11.30pm. Closed Sundays.   5,000 tenge
Italian

With its rustic, Tuscan décor, Pomodoro brings a slice of Italy to central Almaty with the best Italian comfort food in town. Small and homey, it is a family-run restaurant where Chef Patron Giorgio Palazzi greets his regulars

by name and remembers their preferred vintage with his home-made tagliatelle and fresh pesto. Palazzi comes from Le Marche, the truffle capital of Italy, and after the harvest each October, he returns with bundles of fresh, highly prized white truffles to complement his fare. Pomodoro prides itself on serving the freshest ingredients; the mozzarella is made everyday by Italians living in Almaty along with green basil and rocket grown at a nearby *dacha* in the hills. The most decadent side of Pomodoro, though, reveals itself on the dessert menu – Palazzi's own *abbracio*, a tantalizing combination of *zabaione* custard and hot chocolate is a tasting delight for any culinary aficionado. Pomodoro will temporarily move from its current location in May/June 2008 for renovation but will return shortly thereafter.

Food 9, Service 9, Atmosphere 7

Porto Maltese, 109 Panfilov St (Gogol), Almaly
Tel: 273 2178
Open: daily, noon–11pm   9,000 tenge
Fish/Seafood

A restaurant devoted entirely to fish in Kazakhstan, the world's largest double land-locked country, may seem incongruous, but that is exactly what Porto Maltese is, and what a joy! Pick your fish from the counter at the front of the restaurant, and then choose from a variety of cooking methods such as 'grilled', 'in salt', 'in bergamot pepper', 'steamed' or 'fried'. You can choose from mullet, sole, dorado, sea bass, john dory, turbot... the list goes on. Also delicious is the seafood risotto and the rocket salad with octopus

and mushrooms for starters. A great place to come to for either lunch or dinner and relax in the nautically themed interior whose simplicity could come straight from the shores of the Mediterranean. The waiters, in long blue aprons, look as if they come fresh from a seafood market, although in reality they're Serbian. They will serve and debone your fish at your table, and are happy to recommend wines to complement your meal.

Food 8, Service 8, Atmosphere 7

Primavera, Koktem Business Centre, 180 Dostyk Avenue (Zholdasbekov), Medeu
Tel: 237 5087
Open: daily, noon–midnight   8,500 tenge
Fusion

Take the elevator to the thirteenth floor of the Koktem (Kazakh for spring) Business Centre, and step into Primavera – a giant glass globe with one of Almaty's most stunning panoramas. Best viewed at sunset (but lovely, too,

when the city is lit up at night), Primavera boasts unrestricted views over the Compote neighborhood and Koktubey television tower to the east, the Tien Shan Mountains to the south and the northerly steppe. Handsomely decorated with crocodile-skin wall coverings, crushed velvet chairs and oversized doorways, Primavera has a New York penthouse feel, making it a perfect spot for a quiet lunch meeting or a more intimate evening away. The refreshingly short menu of European and Japanese-fusion cuisine offers diverse dishes, such as foie gras on apple gratin with crimson sauce and venison or duck served with wood mushrooms that are complemented by an impressive wine list chosen by the restaurant's very own wine club.

Food 7, Service 6, Atmosphere 8

Sadu Concept Store, Mercur Town, Samal 3/25 (Furmanov), Samal Microdistrict
Tel: 271 6865
Open: daily, noon–midnight   6,500 tenge
Mediterranean

This restaurant/boutique is the last word in convenience store, combining lunch or dinner with shopping for the latest fashions from experimental designers in the adjoining boutique. With its green- and brown-striped chairs and menus, olive sofas and soothing earth tones, the cool interior of

this sunlit restaurant is a welcome contrast to the heat of an Almaty summer.

Attracting an older, more elite crowd, Sadu's Italian chef Simone makes simple but delicious Mediterranean dishes, including a variety of hand-made pastas and sauces (you can choose your favourite combination) and to complete the meal, his very own *limoncello*. No visit to Sadu is complete, however, without trying one of their unique fresh energy, cleansing, health promoting or aphrodisiac juices. The ingredients of each juice are spelled out and the properties of each ingredient listed underneath.

Food 7, Service 9, Atmosphere 7

Safran, 36 Dostyk Avenue (Bogenbai), Medeu
Tel: 293 8667 or 293 8383
Open: daily, noon (1pm Sun)–midnight   9,000 tenge
Middle Eastern

At night, this Middle Eastern style restaurant is illuminated to reveal a white façade covered in Arabic script that lures diners inside to sample its mix of Moroccan, Turkish and Georgian cuisine. Dotted with Islamic-style accents and incense-scented air, Safran is popular in the evening when dishes, such as the lamb served in a *tagine* with dried fruits and chestnuts on saffron rice

and salmon-spinach falafel rolls served with *wasabi* and *tahini* sauce, fill the tables of those searching for something a little more exotic. Be sure to sample Safran's own version of the famous Turkish dish, *Imam Bayildi*, and complete your meal with their Arabic coffee, a special recipe blended with cardamom and *harissa* and served with a pitcher of mint-flavoured water. No trip to Safran is complete without a visit to the loo (once hired out to film a music video) where mosque lanterns and ornately tiled walls make one wish the design had been extended to the rest of the restaurant.

Food 7, Service 7, Atmosphere 6

Sapphire Lounge Restaurant, 29/3 Satpaev St (Baitursynuly), Bostandyk
Tel: 260 6767
Open: noon–2am Mon–Fri; 6pm–4am Sat and Sun   5,000 tenge
Chinese

The name alone conjures up images of decadence and glitz, so you can only imagine what's in store once you arrive. A rather unassuming building from the outside, Sapphire's main hallway is elaborately decorated with all things Asian; Chinese designs sit next to traditional Islamic arches accented by neon-coloured and spray-painted desert scenes that glow in the dark. Losing oneself in a fantasy world doesn't take long – especially not after a sumptuous dinner of authentic Chinese cuisine. Sapphire is most popular among a younger (16–25) and very wealthy crowd. In fact, sometimes the cars parked outside rival those at L'Affiche (see Snack). For these young hipsters, the *kalyan* (water pipe) is all the rage; they'll lie for hours smoking and drinking and occasionally get up to dance to the resident DJ's Asian lounge, chill-out and R&B tunes. Uber-friendly manager Sheikh Saif is always on hand, and it's best to ring him in advance for reservations.

Food 7, Service 8, Atmosphere 7

Sumo San, 159 Baitursynuly St, Bostandyk
Tel: 292 8738 or 292 2586
Open: daily, noon–midnight   5,000 tenge
Japanese

Situated around the corner from the InterContinental Hotel, Sumo San is a favourite with Japanese expatriates living in Almaty. This patronage is borne out by attentive service (at the end of a bell), an extensive menu including both *sushi* and *teppyanaki* and an owner who, although Kazakh, is head of the Kazakhstan Sumo Association. Photos of sumo wrestlers greet you as you enter this friendly restaurant with its rabbit warren of rooms.

Decorated in a homely fashion with two earth-coloured *tatami* rooms and large for-mat photo-graphs of Mount Fuji and details of Japanese Cherry blos-som dominating the main hall, Sumo San is a relaxed and tasty place to have a *bento* lunch for 800 to 2,200 tenge including *miso* soup and a drink. In summer, the outside terrace partitioned by reed screens and bamboo also makes for intimate dining.

Food 7, Service 7, Atmosphere 7

Thai, 50 Dostyk Avenue (Kurmangazy), Medeu
Tel: 291 0910
Open: daily, noon–11pm   6,500 tenge
Thai

You may not associate horsemeat with Thai food but at the Thai Restaurant in Almaty, when wrapped in *pandan* leaves, it is a perennial favourite. For

those of you who prefer more traditional dishes, the *Tom Yam Goong* (spicy prawn & lemongrass soup) and the *Tom Kha Gai* (chicken & coconut milk soup) are highly recommended. The menu is easy to navigate with each page based on a main ingredient, such as snowfish, mussels, lobster and even kobe beef, followed by eight different ways of eating it. With chefs from Thailand and delicacies imported daily from all over the world, you can't beat Thai for authentic flavour and freshness. Thanks to attentive waiters who speak English, relaxing in this funky art deco restaurant isn't hard. But the Asian fusion doesn't stop there. The rear of the restaurant houses 'Zen' – a minimalist Japanese *sushi* and *sashimi* bar, with mouthwatering *maki* and *sushi*. Centrally located next to the Hotel Kazakhstan, this restaurant is, quite simply, a must.

Food 9, Service 9, Atmosphere 8

Zheti Kazyna, 58a Ablai Khan Avenue (entrance on Makatayev), Zhetisu

Tel: 273 2587

Open: daily, noon–midnight   8,000 tenge

Central Asian, Chinese and Russian

Zheti Kazyna (meaning Seven Treasures) is a definite case of three for the price of one. Welcomed at the door by a Kazakh *apa* or grandmother, you are asked to state your preference for Eastern, European and Russian, or Oriental cuisine. Depending on your answer, you will then be led into one of three restaurants on the premises (although you can order from any of

the three menus wherever you end up). To the left is Zheti Kazyna, an Uzbek-styled restaurant with an open tiled kitchen running down one side, beautifully carved Uzbek columns holding up painted ceilings, marble fountains between the tables and arched windows with *paranjas* (latticed screens with a geometric design) overlooking the summer terrace. The local Kazakh, Uzbek, Uighur and Dungan food here takes a lot of beating. The *besparmak* (which means five fingers in Kazakh), the Kazakh national dish made with meat and ribbons of home-made pasta, is mouthwateringly delicious here, as are the *samsa* with spinach, sorrel and cheese. Through Zheti Kazyna to the right is Caramel, an elegantly decorated restaurant with marble floors and William Morris style wallpaper, where each table has its own harlequin set of chairs – be they red velvet, upholstered in chintz or black pony-skin sofas. This is definitely a place for formal dining and the menu, with dishes such as rocket with foie gras and strawberries, or venison *palmeni* and cedarnuts braised in cream with cheese, complements the refined atmosphere, as does the faultless, if ocassionally over-attentive, service.

Downstairs is Zi, an oriental emporium serving Japanese and Chinese food. Walk along a purple corridor with oriental clouds painted onto the red ceiling and a dragon looping its way over the doors giving onto a variety of intimate, oriental style rooms with round tables and lazy susans. Or choose a *tatami* style room where you sit on the floor and the waitresses come in on their knees. If you are feeling truly over the top, you can give 24 hours notice, pay in advance, and order *flash sushi*, in which case your sushi will be served on a naked woman – art apparently.

Food 9, Service 8, Atmosphere 8

Zontiki, 44 Kurmangazy Street (Tulebaev), Medeu
Tel: 272 6759 or 272 6755
Open: daily, 11am–midnight   5,600 tenge
Japanese/Korean

Zontiki translates as parasol (or umbrella), a fact alluded to in the miminalist interior of this restaurant in the form of cream and orange parasol lampshades hanging from the pale wooden walls and ceiling. The fresh, light interior of Zontiki makes it an extremely pleasant place to while away the evening, and if you like classic pop songs, so much the better. Zontiki's Korean chef cooks up a variety of Japanese and Korean food. The sushi

arrives on a wooden boat and, as at Korea House, if you order Korean food you will be treated to delicious Korean *kimchi* (or starters) for free. When you finish, try some *kadury* with your tea – a sweet Korean rice cake with toasted sesame seeds and honey, or splash out on the eponymous Umbrella Cake. Be warned though, that because this restaurant is connected to the Dom Priomov or House of Receptions, a vast building that you can hire out for banquets, weddings, balls etc., the restaurant is occasionally commandeered on a Saturday night, so it is best to ring in advance.

Food 7, Service 7, Atmosphere 6

Notes & Updates

drink...

The latest drink to hit the bars and clubs of Europe and America is Snow Queen – a deliciously pure Kazakh vodka drunk by all the right people in all the right places (thanks to a concerted marketing effort). In Almaty, the best place to get onto the Snow Queen bandwagon is at Vogue Bar on the corner of Satpaev and Furmanov, as fashionable as its name suggests.

Kazakhstan's vodka drinking culture arrived with the Russians over 150 years ago, and despite the nominally Islamic nature of the country, the drink has proved popular. Vodka, be it Snow Queen or something other, is best drunk in shots accompanied by hearty toasts, and is probably preferable to the traditional Kazakh drink, *kumiss*, or fermented mare's milk.

Vodka shots aside, a transformation is taking place in Almaty. With the opening of a handful of new lounge bars, long drinks and cocktails are taking off. It's not unusual to see long-legged Kazakh beauties sipping mojitos before taking their Manolos for a spin on the dance floor. The cocktail revolution really came to town, though, with the opening of Boudoir in August 2007, a lounge restaurant with a cocktail menu created by a London mixologist. His combinations of local

ingredients and heady liqueurs have produced some of the best cocktails we've ever tasted... anywhere.

Bars in the traditional sense, however, simply do not exist. Everywhere listed here also serves food and most of the places listed are open at lunchtime as well as in the evening. If you just want a beer and a plate of chips (as opposed to something fancier) and want to catch up with some expats, note that Almaty has a wide selection of pubs. We've included one – Line Brew – because it has the best selection of Belgian beer in the country, but there are others including Guinness, Mad Murphy's, Dublin and Glenn Pub. Alternatively, you could head for Soho – a popular destination for both expats and locals, which is one of the liveliest places around on a Friday night.

A note of warning: people in Kazakhstan get dressed up to go out. Walk along the streets of Almaty and you will notice that most Kazakh women are dressed as if they are going to a cocktail party, even if they are going to get a pint of milk. Unless you've packed a stash of your designer finest, be prepared to feel like a country bumpkin in many of the bars we recommend.

If you really want to splash out, why not go bling with a bottle of Louis Roederer Cristal 1999? At one lounge bar, La Fete, it is listed on the menu at $2,000 a bottle and apparently they've sold four bottles so far. Now see if you can top that!

Boudoir, 134 Bogenbai Batyr (Ablai Khan), Almaly
Tel: 272 5555
Open: daily, noon–2am

The cocktails in this lounge/restaurant are out of this world. Created by a London mixologist, they are either a perfect complement to the global fusion cuisine, or worth a visit in their own right. Using as many local ingredients as possible, the list includes 'The Big Apple' – fresh Almaty apples

smashed with sage and shaken with vanilla infused vodka and sour apple liqueur, or 'Unbeetable', which combines gin with beetroot, thyme, passion fruit syrup and apple juice. Only recently opened, the sophisticated local crowd is beating a path to Boudoir's shiny black marbled door. So why not join them and pop in for an 'Essex Girl' or a pair of 'Gucci Shoes'.

Cinzano, 109b Dostyk Avenue (Kazhymukan), Medeu
Tel: 253 1345
Open: daily, noon–8am

By day you can eat a sushi lunch at Cinzano for 1,500 tenge in the calm, hip surroundings of either Cinzano's white Bianca room, red Rossa room overlooked by three large pictures of Marilyn Monroe, or the dark terrace with a wall of windows looking out onto the street. Cross the 9pm watershed, however, and Cinzano is where the bright young things hang out, sipping at cocktails with names like Cocaine, Break Point, Toxic and Sin through straws. With 130 different types of cocktail, and an achingly cool reputation, it can be hard to get in to Cinzano, although with its late opening hours, it's

a good place to come if you want to carry on drinking after a night of club-bing. From Thursday to Saturday DJ Mora pumps out suitably hip tunes, and with a battery of seven shots costing just 3,000 tenge, drinking can get com-petitive. The extensive menu of flavoured ice teas, non-alcoholic cocktails (such as 'Safe Sex on the Beach') and milkshakes is probably best tested before that watershed.

Di Wang Lounge Bar, 75 Zhambyl Street (Tschaikovskovo), Almaly

Tel: 272 3810 www.diwang.kz
Open: 9pm–last customer Thursday–Saturday

Di Wang is a favourite restaurant by night (see Eat) and a favourite lounge bar into the early hours. Start with a *kalyan* in Di Wang's 'red room', accent-ed with thick red pillars and lotus images under dim lighting, before

descending the stairs to the lounge bar where the exquisitely minimal design, low-slung beige couches, and wide bamboo partitions encourage you to relax the night away to the DJ's chill-out, lounge music. Di Wang's sleek red chairs provide the perfect vantage point from where to watch (with a cocktail or two from the opaque, white illuminated bar) Almaty's sophisticated and stylish, who come here to be seen. Di Wang is serious about its music – inviting world-class DJs to spin the nights away. Claude and Jean-Marc Challe and DJ Ravin (of Buddha Bar fame) as well as the UK's Gentle People have all graced Di Wang's decks.

Fame, 115/5 Bogenbai Batyr (Tulebaeva), Medeu
Tel: 244 9627 or 244 9629
Open: daily, noon–last customer

Opened in 2007, this bar/restaurant has become an instant hit with the stylish local elite. Tucked behind the Grand Tien Shan Hotel, Fame's elegant chocolate minimalist style is undeniably cool, with photos of Paul Newman, Audrey Hepburn, Steve McQueen and other Hollywood stars providing a hall of fame as you walk in. In fact, this place is so opulent that even the

ubiquitous flatscreen TV is in a gold frame. Discreet lounge music filters through the speakers, except on Friday nights in summer when it's time to party to a DJ playing electro-house. If you want to relax, find the cozy summer terrace with low tables and cushioned wicker chairs – the perfect place to try one of Fame's 'famed' fruit sorbets. Usually open late into the night, Fame is a great place to pop into for an after-dinner drink, where you can prop up the piano-key-edged bar.

La Fete, 44 Kurmangazy Street (Furmanov, downstairs in the Hall of Receptions building), Medeu
Tel: 272 7837 or 272 7883
Open: daily, 6pm–2am

Like Zontiki (see Eat), La Fete is attached to the Dom Priomov or House of Receptions, although you don't have to come from a Viennese Ball upstairs to get in. Situated in the basement, La Fete is a cavernous lounge bar with its own house DJ playing 'light' house music. Most of the customers tend to sit and drink in the lounge area beneath paintings of the French partying circa 1920, hence the name. To be truly decadent, you could order a bottle of Louis Roederer Cristal here for $2,000. Originally created in 1876 for Tsar Alexander II, this could be the heftiest price tag commanded for champagne in this town, although if you do take the plunge, know that you won't be the first to have done so. Flamboyant hedonism is rampant in Almaty.

Line Brew, 187 Furmanov Street (Abai), Bostandyk
Tel: 250 7985
Open: daily, noon–last customer

Something of a rarity in Kazakhstan, Line Brew has been open for almost 10 years. Officially calling itself a beer restaurant, we thought it merited inclusion here for having the largest selection of Belgian beer in the country. Line Brew is the upmarket version of the Irish/English/Scottish pub, of which there are many in Almaty. Set in a mock Gothic-style Belgian castle with exposed brick walls and stained-glass windows, Line Brew's dark wood tables and benches are the place to come if you want to choose from a wide selection of beers such as Leffe, Abbey De and Delirium Tremens. With each beer meriting a page of explanation in the drinks menu, this is definitely a place for connoisseurs. The other real attraction is the *mangal* or open fire where the chef cooks up delicious *shashlyk* and steak in front of you. In summer the fire is transferred to the attractive summer terrace on the roof, dominated by a tall sailing ship in full sail – the perfect spot for live musicians to strut their stuff. In winter, an elegant

navy and neutral Italian restaurant – Pasta Basta – opens in the basement.

Major, 43 Kazhymukan St (Furmanov), Medeu
Tel: 264 5500
Open: daily, noon–2am

Major (pronounced ma-jour), which calls itself a lounge-restaurant, pulls in a young and trendy crowd at the weekends, starting from 6pm onwards when

the happy hour (which lasts until 8pm) means 30% off anything on the menu. On Friday and Saturday nights, toe-tapping live music (either jazz or a lady singing classic pop songs) makes this a fun place to be, although don't come here for an intimate conversation with a friend – the decibel level is high. If you feel like eating, you'll find the tasty fusion menu and salads, which come in large glass bowls, are delicious. Major is good for a quick *kalyan* or cocktail before going on to a club – or even next door to Ataka – an attractive (if that's not an oxymoron) billiards club where VIP rooms with private billiard tables cost 2,000 tenge an hour. In summer, Major has a large summer terrace overflowing with buddleia, and upstairs is the ever so slightly pretentious restaurant Royal, whose faux classical friezes look down on you as you dine on duck, quail, pheasant and goose or pick from their selection of malt whiskies and fine liqueurs.

Nirvana Bar, Building 2, Dostyk Avenue (Satpaev), Samal Microdistrict

Tel: 264 7450
Open: daily, noon–midnight

While we haven't been to Nirvana Bar yet (it's set to open in October 2007 just before our publication), the name alone has all the trappings of a decadent haunt. Buddha once said that, 'Nirvana is the highest happiness'; he must have been on to something because Nirvana is using the four ele-

ments of life (air, fire, water and earth) to create a restaurant and lounge bar that is a sanctuary of calm and an escape from the hustle of the outside world. Nirvana's DJ will spin lounge tunes while its chef dishes up Chinese and Hong Kong cuisine. Meanwhile, you're invited to sit back, relax and start your own journey to nirvana. (Opening hours are likely to be extended once Nirvana has been open for some time, so if you're looking for a little bit of heaven after midnight, be sure to check out Nirvana.)

Oxa Lounge Bar, 67a Gabdullin St (Auezov), Bostandyk
Tel: 275 6253
Open: daily, 6pm–5am

Newly renovated in autumn 2007, Oxa Lounge Bar (on the western edge of the Business District) keeps its well-to-do mid-20-to-30-something crowd grooving all night long with its low-key glamour. No matter your mood, Oxa has something for you: Wednesday nights are retro (that means 1980s tunes), Thursday is R&B, and Friday is house night, when Oxa invites local

DJs to spin their own. No Almaty club repertoire would be complete without an 'Erotic Show', so Saturday is when Oxa's striptease lets the girls go wild. If you're lucky, you might catch Orda, Kazakhstan's very own boy band, which puts the Backstreet Boys to shame. Even if boy bands aren't your thing, Orda puts on such a great show that it keeps the place buzzing all night. Downstairs, Dibo Bar is open 24 hours – an easy option if you're not quite ready to go home when Oxa spins its last tune.

Posh Bar, Mercur Town, 3/25 Al-Farabi (Furmanov), Samal
Tel: 266 3996
Open: daily, 9am–last guest

Located on the ground floor of one of the three Mercur towers on Al-Farabi, Posh Bar lives up to its name with some of the smoothest locals in town regularly crossing the threshold. With a new 'New York chic' interior being unveiled in November 2007, Posh is sure to be busy. Unlike most bars, Posh opens at 9am, offering breakfast to their hungover clientele. During the day, Posh attracts a sleek business crowd who come for the free WiFi and

groovy atmosphere. From 5pm to 6pm it's teatime and then, in the evening, the bar takes over. On Fridays and Saturdays the resident DJ will play light house and lounge music, and a new dance pole is sure to be a popular attraction. Age and face control will be applied, though, so make sure you dress up to the nines if you want to get in.

Soho, 65 Kazibek Bi Street (Furmanov), Almaly
Tel: 267 0367   www.soho.kz
Open: daily, 9am–3am

Like its namesakes in New York and London, Soho is a lively place to hang-out any night of the week. With live music from 9pm daily, Soho's dance floor is usually packed as people dance to one of three bands playing jazz, retro, 1980s music and classics such as the Beatles, the Rolling Stones and … AC/DC. The crowd is mixed, consisting in large part of expats (usually men) who come to drink and socialize at the pub-like bar. But there are also lots of Kazakhs here, some on the arms of the expat men, and others just enjoying the vibrant atmosphere. In summer Soho doubles in size, but still manages to burst at the seams as people smoke, drink and dance their way

through the evening. With a wide range of bar food, tex-mex and even a full English breakfast menu, Soho caters to all tastes.

Stylish Dog, Café Max Internet-Centre, 1A Timiryazev St, Bostandyk
Tel: 260 9888 www.cafemax.kz
Open: daily, noon–midnight

A stone's throw from the InterContinental Hotel, Stylish Dog is located above the Café Max Internet Centre at the beginning of Timiryazev St. It may seem an unlikely place for a lounge bar, but it works. The name Stylish Dog refers to the @ symbol used in email addresses, which in Russian translates as 'little dog', and consequently the symbol pops up throughout the bar. At lunchtime (2–4pm) you can get a *bento* box from 1,200 tenge, while in the evening the over 25s come to relax before going clubbing. With

its white leather armchairs and trendy design features, the overhanging blossom lights and fluorescent table legs filled with bubbling water, Stylish Dog lives up to its name, and it couldn't be more convenient if you need to check your email. On Fridays and Saturdays DJs play chill-out music from the decks next to the bar.

Tinkoff, 27a Satpaev Street (Masanchi), Bostandyk
Tel: 292 4900 www.tinkoff.ru
Open: daily, noon–2am

This four-storey complex in a stand-alone building halfway between the Hyatt and the InterContinental is a lively hangout and micro-brewery. The large aluminium casks, in which the house beer is brewed, decorate the glass

and steel industrial interior. Spaced out over four floors, the top floor makes a fantastic roof terrace in the summer and the second floor offers live Latino music from 10pm to midnight. Tinkoff is also a great place to eat, with European and Japanese cooking complementing the home-made beer. If you're in the mood try the beer cocktails – Black Velvet (a combination of beer and champagne) and the Red Eye (a take on a Bloody Mary with tomato juice, spices and Pilsner beer). Tinkoff has a large capacity, but always manages to be full, possibly because it is more democratic than some of its fancier counterparts, attracting a lively, middle-class crowd.

Vitalita, 63 Tole Bi Street (Zheltoksan), Almaly
Tel: 272 7461
Open: daily, 10am–last guest

Vitalita is located in the basement of the building on the northeast corner of Tole Bi and Zheltoksan at the bottom of a set of white marble stairs. Open the door at the weekend and you step into a world of chicly dressed girls in their Jimmy Choos dancing to the resident DJ who plays R&B and dance music on Wednesday, Friday and Saturday nights from 9pm onwards. Opened in September 2006, Vitalita appears to be standing the test of time

and attracts a youngish crowd. This may have something to do with the cool interior, with its illuminated bar, cosmopolitan white and chocolate brown leather seats, low lighting and columns draped in chiffon. You can either arrive early and choose from an Italian menu or pop in later to sip a few cocktails.

Vogue Bar, 11 Satpaev Street (Furmanov), Medeu
Tel: 264 1699
Open: daily, 11am–3am

A visit to Vogue Bar is not to be missed for a sample of barman Sasha's luscious long drinks. Voted Kazakhstan's Champion Barman, as well as the winner of numerous other mixology matches, Sasha pours a mean mojito and has an extensive portfolio of cocktails ready to be sipped. Try his Ruby Crush (orange, grapefruit, lime, vodka and mandarin syrup) and then settle back into Vogue's plush seats to watch Sasha shake his stuff during Friday night's weekly Barman Show, while the resident DJ spins house and

progressive tunes on Friday and Saturday nights. Lipstick red is the understandable theme inside Vogue, and its smaller size creates a warm and cozy atmosphere, often lost in some of Almaty's larger bars, making Vogue the kind of place in which you might find yourself still sipping at into the wee hours of the morning.

snack...

Almaty is a city on the cusp of a coffee revolution. Cafés are beginning to pop up everywhere, and while coffee is still not that popular, it is becoming more so. Often, though, you will find the locals at coffee shops drinking tea, with milk if they are Kazakh, or with a spoonful of jam or a slice of lemon if they are Russian.

Younger locals like to hang out at Biscvit or Coffeedelia, a large American-style coffee shop that has done phenomenally well and is soon to open a smaller, cosier branch at Bogenbai Batyr and Zheltoksan. Older, more sophisticated locals head for Bon Bon for its famed tiramisu, but if you're looking for tasty cakes or a simple sandwich to go with your coffee, look no further than 4A, just off the Arbat – a family-run coffee shop owned by an American expat and his Kazakh wife serving delicious American-style muffins and home-roasted coffee.

If you want to try, and or buy, a wide variety of tea and coffee, check out Tea and Coffee Garden on Zheltoksan, just opposite the Ambassador Hotel, or John's Coffee on Satpaev, perfectly situated if you need a break from one of the main hotels in the Business District.

Almaty also has a number of European-style cafés serving food and alcohol which are almost indistinguishable from bars or restaurants. The best of these is

L'Affiche (left), a bistro café opposite the Opera House attracts the smartest clientele in Almaty, the perfect place to begin or end an evening at the opera.

Cafés are also a great place to get connected as more and more offer WiFi, usually free except for in the hotels. You may have problems getting online if you have a Mac, although now that the first Apple Store has opened in Kazakhstan, their rising popularity as the must-have machine should change that.

And finally, if you want to get away from the smoky atmosphere, why not head for a light Indian snack at Govinda's – a café run by the Hare Krishna community which steers clear of alcohol, cigarettes, meat, fish and even onions and garlic.

4A Coffee, 81 Zhibek Zholy (turn right at Altyn Gold Shop on the Arbat just before Tsum), Almaly

Tel: 273 1181   www.4acoffee.com
Open: daily, 8am–9pm (10pm Fri–Sat)

Every once in a while even the most dedicated party animal needs a quiet, unassuming and completely relaxing place to recover and here it's 4A

Coffee. Opened in February 2007, 4A Coffee is one of the best things to have hit Almaty in a long time. Run by an American and his Kazakh wife, they decided it was time the traditionally tea-drinking Kazakhs started to learn the finer points of coffee. 4A's homely atmosphere and super friendly staff are a reflection on the owners who can be seen roasting their beans from 12 different countries every day. Not only does 4A have some of the freshest coffee in town, but they have finally introduced a proper sandwich to Almaty; a simple selection of tuna, egg salad, chicken, and ham and cheese are a welcome relief to those who have spent endless meals in search of the simple lunch solution.

Biscvit, 18 Shevchenko St (Dostyk), Medeu

Tel: 291 6692 or 293 8284
Open: daily, 8am (10am Sat–Sun)–1am

Biscvit, one of Almaty's original coffee houses, has been a popular spot ever since its doors first opened in 2005. Often described as *demokraticheski* by locals, Biscvit attracts a slightly older and well-rounded segment of Almaty's

coffee-drinking strata – as opposed to the younger, trendier crowd at Coffeedelia and the more *elitni* scene at Bon Bon. Biscvit's atmosphere is laid back and inviting, and it is always full in the evening. A popular breakfast spot, especially in the summer when the sidewalk café is open, diners choose from English, Russian, traditional or continental breakfast selections. Biscvit's coffee menu includes all the standard fare, as well as designer coffees like the Banana Split that are perfect with their fresh cakes and pastries. Sandwiches and pasta dishes are available as well as free WiFi; just ask a waiter for the daily password and they'll provide instructions on how to connect.

Bon Bon, 123 Ablai Khan Avenue (Zhambul), Almaly
Tel: 261 1739
Open: daily, 11am–midnight

Bon Bon offers a classic little French café in central Almaty for a more sophisticated and mature clientele. Decorated with antique French posters, the light, airy atmosphere is the perfect place to catch up with friends. Bon Bon only brews Pellini coffee and boasts a menu with an impressive selection of black, white and green teas. Be sure to try the Japanese Linden – a refreshing green tea with Japanese Linden flowers, Chinese Schizandria, camomile flowers and lemon. In winter, warm up over a steaming cup of hot chocolate and feed your soul with any of their delicious, home-made sweets; the pastry shelves are always full of brownies, lemon pie, tiramisu and Linzer tarts. A café menu is also available listing omelettes, soups, salads and sandwiches. If you're in the mood for a more intimate experience, check

out the Middle Eastern room downstairs, complete with plush cushions and *kalyans* (water pipesttt).

Borodino Coffee Shop, 80 Shevchenko St, Almaly
Tel: 272 5201 or 272 8678 www.borodino.kz
Open: daily, 24 hours

Named after the eponymous Napoleonic battle in Russia in 1812, the Borodino Coffee Shop tries to capture the elegance of a 19th-century Napoleonic drawing room, albeit with reproduction furniture and cod por-

traits. Part of a larger complex which houses a restaurant and several VIP dining rooms, the coffee shop is to the right as you enter through the main door. The beauty of Borodino, though, is that it is open 24 hours a day, and the perfect place to pop in to during the winter if you need to recharge your batteries, want a hot chocolate, or need somewhere to read *War and Peace* in peace. Although not part of the coffee shop, there is a cigar-bar downstairs which has a table with a reconstruction of the Battle of Borodino, and portraits of Napoleon and Marshal Kutuzov hanging on the wall, so if you are an amateur historian or want to see where Pierre Bezuhov stood, why not head on down?

CoffeeDelia, 79 Kabanbai Batyr (Tulebaev), Medeu
Tel: 272 6409 www.coffeedelia.com
Open: 8am–midnight Sun–Thurs; 9am–1am Fri–Sat

WiFi access, jumbo lattes, bright orange and wooden décor, this coffee bar has to be the most popular place in Almaty right now – the place to see and be seen. In fact it is so trendy that unlike Starbucks it stays open well into the night, when it becomes the hangout for the children of the new elite and serves alcohol too. Situated right in the heart of downtown Almaty, the café's motto, 'Love coffee, love people', aptly sums up the feelings

of owner Andrei Chagay who trained as a *barista* in Seattle five years ago and has plans to open a second CoffeeDelia three blocks away. The wide selection of sandwiches, paninis, soups and pizza plus home-baked pastries and croissants make it a popular pop-in joint from breakfast onwards for what always appears to be a mainly Turkish business crowd. In the summer the café spills out onto the pavement and is a great place for people watching as old and new Almaty mix on the street in front.

Govindas, 39 Ablai Khan Avenue (Mametov), Zhetisu
Tel: 271 0836 or 271 3235
Open: daily, noon–9pm

If you're tired of the smokey atmosphere that pervades most of the restaurants, bars and cafés in Almaty, head for Govinda's – a non-smoking, no alcohol, vegetarian café (they don't use eggs, onions or garlic in their food either). Between midday and 3pm you can get a complex lunch for 1,000

tenge which comes in small stainless steel dishes and includes rice, vegetables with *paneer*, *dahl*, bread and a lemon drink and is deliciously refreshing. Run by the local Hare Krishna group, most of the food comes fresh from their farm just outside Almaty, although recent problems with the authorities may force them to move. In the entrance a shop sells incense, spices, Indian ayuverdic cosmetics, oils, jewellery, pashminas and saris, and, should you be interested, information and CDs on the Hare Krishna movement. Note that credit cards are not accepted here.

Grand Café, 149 Furmanov St (Zhambul), Almaly
Tel: 261 2914
Open: daily, 10am–midnight

This European-style café is just a stone's throw from the Opera House and right in the heart of town. Unlike most places the menu is relatively simple offering soups, salads, steaks, pasta and pizza and, our favourite, movenpick ice-cream. From Tuesday to Friday there are the occassional jazz and piano nights, which pick up the atmosphere but be aware they do not run on a

timetable and are unpredictable. The VIP room can be hired for 4,000 tenge an hour and is a comfortable place in which to relax in leather armchairs and smoke a cigar by the fire in the winter.

John's Coffee, 11a Satpayev St (Masanchi), Bostandyk
Tel: 292 5076 www.johnscoffee.com.tr
Open: daily, 8am–11pm

Imagine a Danish coffee-lover living in Turkey introducing the concept of gourmet coffee, and it suddenly takes off. Not long afterwards, he's got a successful chain of coffee shops with the newest one recently opened in Almaty's Business District. John's Coffee is a quick and easy café much like

one you might frequent in New York or London. Not only is it convenient for those in the Business District, it's also smack in the middle of Almaty's universities with 15,000 students studying nearby. With a small, brightly lit seating area, John's offers a simple selection of breakfasts, sandwiches and desserts – and of course a wide array of piping hot coffees to enjoy inside or on your way to that next meeting. Give their Java Chip Frappe a try, and look for their red sign around town as more branches are set to open.

L'Affiche, 83 Kabanbai Batyr (Panfilov), Almaly
Tel: 272 1092
Open: daily, 11am–2am (4am Fri–Sat)

With its full-panel glass windows, L'Affiche (as its name suggests) offers a poster perfect view of the Abai Opera and Ballet Theatre situated just opposite this chic, European café. During the day, you'll see well-suited busi-

nessmen huddling across the tables to negotiate their latest deal while Gucci and Prada clad ladies-who-lunch chat under the umbrellas of its Parisian-style summer terrace. At night, Bentleys and Mercedes with blacked-out windows wait outside while inside their owners enjoy the elegantly prepared European cuisine. With its painted ceilings depicting scenes from a Gauguin masterpiece and its dark wooden interior, L'Affiche is the perfect spot for a pre-opera champagne or a post-show dinner. Start with blinis and Beluga caviar followed by the sea bass with asparagus and sundried tomatoes or the New Zealand veal and wash it all down with a bottle of Chateau Mouton Rothschild. Be warned, though, the Grand Cru will set you back at least $1,000…

Le Jardin, 10 Satpaev St (Valikhanov), Medeu
Tel: 263 3646, 263 3953 or 262 7683
Open: daily, 11am–11pm

This small café in the midst of Almaty's highest-priced boutiques, and at the northern edge of the Business District, is the perfect spot to rest your heels after a shopping spree at nearby Sauvage or Strenesse (as well as to

recover from sticker shock). Look for the sign on the sidewalk and follow it downstairs to sample some of Le Jardin's European-style home-cooking, including a refreshing selection of salads and local mountain trout. Le Jardin's airy garden atmosphere is complemented with wicker furniture and a floral theme that permeates the café in everything from the upholstery to the flower-decorated ceiling; even the loo paper has its own hanging basket. The attentive service and relaxed atmosphere might encourage you to sit back and lose yourself in the pages of one of the many books that line the walls, although most are in Russian. For the faster paced, internet access is available for a nominal fee.

Tea and Coffee Garden, 132 Zheltoksan St (Karasai Batyr), Almaly
Tel: 272 3257, 272 6140 or 272 5168
Open: daily, 10am–11pm

Located just opposite the Ambassador Hotel, it's hard to miss the fresh smell of tea and coffee wafting from this tiny café. Tea and Coffee Garden is Almaty's first genuine tea shop offering more than 100 types of tea from

around the world. The knowledgeable *baristas* can recommend a tea for any occasion – be it white, green, red, black, fruity, or herbal from India, Japan, China, Africa or Mexico. Similarly, their selection of 20 different coffees is roasted on the premises. The café is decorated with the steeping and brewing accoutrements, as if you're inside an old Chinese teashop with hundreds of antique tea canisters adorning the wall – making your sipping selection tantalizingly difficult. Tea and Coffee Garden offers a similar light café menu to other places in town, but it has a unique sense of charm and coziness that offers an unexpected haven.

Teatralnaya, 51A Zhambul St (Baisetov), Almaly

Tel: 272 8777

Open: daily, noon–midnight

Set in a quiet location just behind the Abai Opera and Ballet Theatre, Teatralnaya is a great place to come after a night out at the opera. Summer,

however, is when this café really comes into its own when the large terrace opens. White cushions, wicker furniture and an abundance of greenery and fountains combine to create a serene and tranquil environment. A large glass canopy strung with white canvas sails covers most of the terrace to allow al fresco dining even when it rains. In the autumn the action moves back inside the neo-classically decorated restaurant, where live jazz and classical music are on the cards at weekends. The food (displayed on green leather menus covered in old ballet and opera photos) is, surprise surprise, a mixture of European and national cooking, but very tasty. The only complaint is the slow and startled service and a TV the size of a cinema screen, but if you can put up with these, Teatralnaya is a great place to hang out.

Thomi's Pastry, 152 Furmanov St (Kurmangazy), Medeu
Tel: 267 0862 or 267 0869
Open: daily, 9am–11pm

Tried and tested among locals and foreigners alike is Thomi's Pastry. With a bright and sunny atmosphere, Thomi's is a perfect spot for families who want to indulge in an afternoon sweet while the business lunch is popular

among workers in the offices nearby. Thomi's offers freshly baked breads, pastries and cakes that are perfect for takeaway or to enjoy in the newly renovated interior to keep up to date with the numerous cafés sprouting up around town. Located on Furmanov, just a few blocks north of Republican Square, Thomi's is the ideal pit stop on your walking tour of the city. With its window seating, watch the city pass by over a café latte (or something a bit stronger like one of their fruit cocktails) and a warm croissant or pain au chocolat. Try the banana cake or kiwi and raspberry tart, and then walk it off as you continue to explore the city.

party...

In a city where marijuana grows wild on the street, and vodka can cost less than fifty pence a bottle, a good party is not hard to find. Almaty's clubs range from those purely for music lovers, such as Da Freak, which plays a great range of progressive and electro house, to luxurious gastro clubs like Euphoria – one of Almaty's smartest venues, which brings in top international DJs to satisfy its upmarket Kazakh crowd.

There is no shortage of go-go dancers, strip shows or topless nights either. If you're looking for an erotic bar or naked dancing, Almaty is definitely the place for you.

Unlike Moscow, face control is limited. Kazakshtanis are much more concerned with the dress code, so don't turn up to a club in tracksuit or trainers – you won't get in. Most clubs charge an entrance fee, which is marginally smaller for girls, and which can change depending on the day of the week. You will also find that you have to pay for tables in clubs, sometimes an inordinate amount. You can (usually) take the table fee off your bar bill but be prepared to drink a lot to reach that limit though!

The latest thing on the club scene is the *kalyan* or shisha pipe (there is even a club named in honour of one). If you are young, rich and have had a night on the town, then it's likely to have included smoking a *kalyan* at some point. The best *kalyans* can be found at Euphoria, where you can smoke fruit and menthol tobacco over a choice of water, milk, wine or cognac. Very hedonistic!

For live music, many bars and restaurants have shows, but the best night-time venue is Cuba on Bogenbai Batyr, which has great local jazz on Friday and Saturday nights. Get your blue suede shoes on – dancing is essential.

During the summer months, clubbing leaves the clubs and gravitates north, Ibiza-style, to a number of 'beach' resorts on Lake Kapchagai. Buses leave from various destinations around the city and you can buy your tickets at chains of shops, such as Meloman, a record shop with branches across the city. It's probably best to get a Russian-speaking friend to look up what is going on at www.night.kz or ask at one of the clubs.

If you are a gambler, then Kazakhstan is not currently the place for you. All of the country's casinos were shut down in 2006 pending a move to two special Las Vegas-style gambling zones – one at Kapchagai, north of Almaty and the other at Schuchinsk, near Astana. Many former casinos are now re-emerging as bars or clubs, while the infrastructure for the two gambling zones is slow moving. Kazakhstan's gamblers, meanwhile, have relocated to Bishkek, capital of Kyrgyzstan.

Crystal, 29 Volodarsky Street (Timirayzev), Business District

Tel: 292 3825
Open: 11pm–6am Fri–Sat

Rumour has it that Crystal is looking for a new venue, but until that happens, you will find it in the Business District just a few blocks away from both the Hyatt and the InterContinental hotels. Crystal is one of the few places that actually calls itself an 'elite' nightclub, and their confidence pays off because Crystal attracts the youngsters of Kazakhstan's new rich in droves, with blacked out Land Rovers and Hummers parked precariously on the pavement outside. Face control, as you can imagine, is a must, so dress

up. The interior's lavish gold and plush velvet decor is adorned with reproduction Old Masters on the walls. Because it's only open on Friday and Saturday, Crystal capitalizes on those nights and hosts extravagant themed parties almost every weekend. Entrance costs 3,000 tenge or 5,000 tenge when a party is on, and tables start from $500. Music is a mix of house, techno and R&B, and in summer, the open roof terrace (entry gained through the adjoining building), which in winter houses a Cabaret show, is the closest you can come to partying under the stars.

Da Freak, 40 Gogol St, Panfilov Park, Medeu

Tel: 273 1337   www.dafreakclub.com
Open: midnight–6am Fri–Sat

Regularly played by international DJs from the UK, Germany, Spain and

Russia, Da Freak is popular with a young and hip local audience and show-cases lots of progressive house music. If you're an aficionado of good electro house, breakbeat, techno or just plain house, then this is the place for you. Like most of the clubs in town, there is dress control (no sports

clothes), but apart from that Da Freak is generally democratic and attracts all types – even, occasionally, a bride and groom and their party of friends in full wedding dress. Situated just to the south of Gogol Street in Panfilov Park, on the same axis as Dostyk Street, Da Freak takes up the second floor of a large square building. The main room sticks to techno while the smaller, red room at the top of the stairs plays mellower electro house. To cool off, in the summer at least, there is a large balcony at the back of the main room.

Esperanza, 481 Seifullin Avenue (Raiymbek), Zhetisu
Tel: 299 6699
Open: daily, 10pm–6am

Always packed at the weekends, Esperanza is one of Almaty's top nightspots, maintaining its popularity by catering to all with house, disco, rap, rock and R&B music on offer. The dance-floor is large by club standards and starts heaving at the weekends. The balcony that runs around three sides of the club is, unusually, not just restricted to VIPs, and the comfy sofas there are worth buying a drink to sit in. The large central column in the middle of the dance-floor is, at one foot wide, too large for pole dancing but the go-go dancers on podiums make up for any disappointment, as does the Erotic Bar next door. The word on the town is that ladies of the night have been

banned from Esperanza; whether this is true or not, it hasn't kept the punters away. Entrance fees vary from free to 500 tenge for women, and free to 2,000 tenge for men; age control is applied in the sense that no ladies under 18 and no guys under 25 are allowed in.

Euphoria, 29/6 Satpaev St (next to the Hyatt Hotel), Bostandyk
Tel: 226 1808
Open: 5pm–2am (5am Thurs–Sat). Closed Sundays.

Euphoria is Almaty's most decadent and glitzy club. Opened in 2007 to much acclaim, from Monday to Wednesday Euphoria works as a simple lounge restaurant, but come Thursday at 11.30pm the nightclub kicks in. Euphoria oozes glamour and with its main VIP room costing 500,000 tenge

(for which you get a huge dining table and private bar in an upstairs room overlooking the entire club) it's obvious that this club is designed with the glitterati in mind. The décor confirms this with swish black and white chandeliers twinkling above shiny monotone surfaces and fancy leather bar stools lining the bar. A cast iron balcony running along the two sides of the central dance-floor is the perfect place to people watch, but beware of those table prices if you want to sit down. Adjacent to the Hyatt Hotel, it couldn't be easier to get to Euphoria if you've decided to take the five-star option. Just make sure you dress up to the nines to get in.

Fashionbar, 61 Masanchi St (Kabanbai Batyr), Almaly
Tel: 292 2566
Open: daily, 6pm–last guest

It might be part of a corporate chain, but you never can tell what will make a bar a hit. In this case, popular patrons and enough scantily clad girls ensure that Fashionbar is the place to be seen drinking on a Friday night, whether expat or local. Opened at the beginning of 2006, Fashionbar's interior combines soft pinks and purples with dalmation print cushions and pink diamond shaped (and encrusted) menus, but what makes it a true Fashionbar is the ubiquitous Fashion TV played continuously on small screens along the

bar and on the walls. The Pretty Woman on the cocktail menu alludes, we imagine, to the hordes of them hanging around the bar. At weekends, the resident DJ is often replaced by big outside names when Fashionbar hosts sumptuously themed parties. If there's a party going on, you have to pay to enter, but otherwise it's free – the only condition being that you look hot. Two new additions to Fashionbar's repertoire are the Italian Fellini restaurant on the ground floor and a drag show on Tuesday nights aimed to appeal to Almaty's fashionable bisexual crowd.

Gas, 100 Seifullin Avenue (Shevchenko), Almaly
Tel: 272 7474
Open: 10pm–6am (7am Weds, 9am Sat). Closed Tuesdays.

Located through the same entrance as neighbouring Petroleum, Gas is a completely separate club and, apart from the name, couldn't be more different. For starters, Gas draws a much younger local crowd than its neighbour, although men (not women) have to be over 21 to get in. With its industrial-style exposed-brick interior and steel-clad columns, Gas is, let's face it, both

stylish and cool. The red tables and modish bar stools overflow with the It Crowd who turn up at the weekends to dance to the club's progressive house music. To keep things buzzing at the beginning of the week, Gas puts on a striptease show on Mondays and invites topless go-go dancers to strut their stuff on Wednesdays. So, apart from Tuesday when the club is closed, there's never not a good time to visit.

Metro, 2b Zhandosov Street (Baizakov), Central

Tel: 247 8166 or 247 8156 www.metro-club.kz
Open: daily, noon–5am (7am Fri–Sat)

There isn't anything, it seems, that you can't do at Metro. In addition to the nightclub and restaurant, this mega-complex offers bowling, billiards and a go-cart track, which makes this a great place to come if you are in an active mood. The club itself is like a giant medieval cavern where you have to walk

over a drawbridge and past a suit of armour to get in. The dance-floor fans out from the restaurant's tables (which cost 10,000 tenge up front) and are arranged in such a way that everybody has a great view of the club's show, a dance spectacle with a new theme every month that starts daily at 12.15am. At 3am, erotic dancers strut their stuff looking for rich men to pay 30,000 tenge for a private dance in one of the small rooms upstairs. Not surprisingly, with all this activity going on, the place is popular with foreigners, and if you prefer disco to house, then this is the place for you.

Most, 12 Kommunalnaya St (Seifullin), Zhetisu

Tel: 233 0457 www.most-club.kz
Open: midnight–9am Fri–Sun

When it's three o'clock in the morning and you've finished at Fashionbar or Euphoria, Most is the place to go. Most, which means bridge, is located between a road and a railway bridge at the bottom of Seifullin Avenue, although the name could refer, more appropriately, to Most's status as a bridge between night and day. Go before 3am and you can dance to the

beat of retro music from the 1980s and 90s. Turn up after 3am and the mainly resident DJs pump out progressive house in the main disco and the adjoining DJ bar. On Thursday nights, DJ Session gives young DJs the opportunity to spin the decks, so if you're into music and want to check out the city's talent, give it a try. Should you get bored of dancing, the entrance to Most is through a giant billiards hall, so you can always pick up a cue instead.

Petroleum, 100 Seifullin Avenue (Shevchenko), Almaly
Tel: 272 7474
Open: daily, 10pm–6am

As you walk up the stairs to this club, you'll notice (if you haven't had one too many vodkas already) that you're winding around the outside of what

looks to be part of an oil rig. Opened long before the actual oil boom came to town, Petroleum is one of Almaty's oldest and most established clubs, offering pop, disco and techno – and the kind of playlist that attracts an older, less music-focused crowd. This explains the proliferation of foreigners and young, pretty local girls who dance the night away in the steel and glass interior…although, perhaps, they are attracted by the free entry before midnight for women (from Monday to Thursday).

Rai, Tselini Cinema, Kabanbai Batyr (Masanchi), Almaly
Tel: 8 701 687 9587
Open: lounge 8pm–6am Thurs–Sat; nightclub 11pm–6am Thurs–Fri

Opened in October 2007, Rai (which means Paradise) is tucked away at the back of the Tselini Cinema on Kabanbai Batyr and Masanchi, a stone's throw from Fashionbar, and… well, equally fashionable. Situated in what was formerly Almaty's most popular nightclub, Heaven, and obviously cashing in on a similar theme, Rai attracts Almaty's most elite and stylish crowd. On the

first floor, an attractively decorated lounge studio with black and white wall-papered walls, long gilt mirrors and decorative lampshades is a great place to sit and people watch. At 11pm, the nightclub upstairs gets going, and the VIP cabins surrounding the dance-floor open for business, but be warned, you'll need to leave a deposit of $1,500 upwards to guarantee a room. Expect good-quality house music, attractive go-go girls, and the opportunity to mingle with the pinnacle of Almaty's fashionable elite.

Shisha Bar, 85 Amangeldi St (Karasai Batyr), Almaly
Tel: 272 8000
Open: daily, 8pm–5am

Entering Shisha is like strolling into an exotic Indian jungle with an Egyptian mummy or two thrown in. Cobras, elephant tusks, images of Buddha and statues of Osiris mingle incongruously among the gyrating bodies of Almaty's IT crowd. VIP sofas visibly sit in the middle of the dance-floor and start at $1,500, which you can recoup by drinking just one bottle of Louis

Roederer Cristal champagne. More VIP rooms line the central balcony upstairs and, downstairs past the statue of Osiris, another VIP zone houses a glass cupboard exclusively for dancing girls. Monday is 1980s disco night, Tuesday is time for an R&B party, and from Wednesday to Sunday DJs such as DJ Sniper, DJ Nikita and DJ Den roll out the house music.

Tornado, Assorti Restaurant, 106G Dostyk Avenue (Abai), Medeu
Tel: 263 3266
Open: 11am–5pm Fri–Sat

We're not quite sure what the name has to do with this nightclub, especially given that the interior is more like an oriental cavern, however, we definitely give Tornado the thumbs up. With a central bar and sofas around the edge of the room, people tend to dance between the two, giving the place a cosy and intimate feel. Golden dragons look on from scarlet walls illuminated by thing Almaty has to a jazz bar with live music every Thursday to Saturday.

Chinese lanterns, which give out a hazy red glow. Tornado regulars tend to be in their 20s and from all walks of life who come together at the weekends to dance to Tornado's two resident DJs, who playing exclusively 1980s retro on Saturdays, and pop, hip-hop and R&B on Fridays. Tornado is part of the Assorti restaurant chain; enter through the restaurant's main door and go up to the third floor to find the club. If you don't find the sofas in Tornado relaxing enough, try the *kalyan* chill-out room next door.

LIVE MUSIC

Bodrum Bar, Ambassador Hotel, 121 Zheltoksan St (Karasai Batyr), Almaly
Tel: 250 8989 or 244 7373 (ask for Bodrum Bar)
Open: daily, 9pm–3am (live music Weds–Sat starting at 1am)

Bodrum Bar, in the basement of the Ambassador Hotel, is possibly one of Almaty's liveliest venues. Its dark, intimate interior attracts many of Almaty's resident Turkish businessmen, as well as hotel guests. What's great about Bodrum is the passionate atmosphere the Turks create. Join in as everyone dances and sings to the live music of Barish and Fatih, the bar's own piano and guitar band that perform a mix of popular Turkish, Russian and English songs to an electrified audience. On weekends, Bodrum Bar broadcasts Turkish football matches and packs the house again with die-hard fans that turn out in support of their favourite teams, although the Galatasaray chant rings through loudest. If all that dancing leaves you a tad hungry, food can

be ordered from Saltanat (the Ambassador's Turkish restaurant with deliciously authentic offerings). Don't miss a visit to Bodrum; it's one of Almaty's few refreshingly local spots.

Cuba, 102 Bogenbai Batyr (Dostyk), Almaly
Tel: 291 2932 or 291 4310
Open: 24 hours daily (Live music Thurs–Sat at 10pm)

Even after a late night on the town, it's not hard to find Cuba; just look for the building with the giant Cuban flag painted on it, and you're there. Step inside the foyer with its Granma-lined ceiling (the official newspaper of Cuba's Communist Party), and old Havana comes alive – exposed brick and dark wood, rattan-style furniture, retro-pewter chandeliers, black and white photos of Cuba on the walls, and even a stained ceiling. Cuba is the closest

Don't miss Almaty's local jazz ensemble, Steps, play on Thursdays and Fridays, as well as Cuba's other live music ranging from blues, Latina, reggae and even African drumming. Once the music starts around 10pm, the dance-floor gets going with Cuba's down-to-earth crowd of locals and foreigners dancing the night away to the salsa or the conga.

STRIP CLUBS

Cacadu Cabaret Club, 122a Ablai Khan Avenue (Abai), Almaly
Tel: 267 3127
Open: daily, 11pm–6am   Entrance: 3,000 tenge

Esperanza Erotic Bar, 481 Seifullin Avenue (Raiymbek), Zhetisu
Tel: 299 6699
Open: daily, 10pm–6am

Stars Club, 171a Zheltoksan St (Abai), Bostandyk
Tel: 261 0744
Open: 10pm–5am Weds–Sun

Sweet & Spice, 34a Abai St, Bostandyk
Tel: 267 5159
Open: daily, 10pm–5am   Entrance: 2,000 tenge

culture...

Almaty is a town with many cultural offerings, but be prepared to dig around to find them. To make things easy, the Central State Museum offers a fascinating insight into the area's rich nomadic heritage. The lack of English signs can be frustrating, but the exquisite quality of nomadic Scythian gold work, for example, needs no translation.

A walk around the town will introduce you to some of Almaty's architectural heritage, from its Russian Orthodox churches and charming painted wooden houses in the outlying areas, to some interesting examples of early Soviet architecture (check out the post office on the corner of Bogenbai Batyr and Ablai Khan designed by the Moscow-based architect Gerasimov). You will walk past numerous statues and monuments to some of Kazakhstan's most famous citizens – writers, musicians, soldiers and heroes.

On the eastern edge of the city, it is well worthwhile taking a walk in the Kensai graveyard – the official burial ground for the Communist elite whose Soviet-style gravestones bear photographic images of the deceased. On a good day the graveyard offers a great view of the mountains as well.

In the Business District, you will find the Kasteyev State Museum of Arts – a two-storey museum with an absorbing collection of Soviet, post-Soviet, European and Russian art.

Kazakhstan's culture also lies in its people. With over 130 different nationalities living in the country, many of whom were transported here on Stalin's orders, you will find a story wherever you turn. Don't be afraid to ask people about

their history, you may find that your Kazakh friend actually has five 'bloods' and an interesting tale to tell into the bargain.

And finally... remember that much of Kazakhstan's heritage, in a society that was formerly nomadic, lies in nature. Go out into the countryside, take a hike from Medeo and before you know it, you will find a yurt and some dogs, and not far away a woman milking a horse to make *kumiss* or fermented mare's milk. Alternatively, drive out into the steppe in search of petroglyphs, ancient rock drawings by nomads from ages past. The culture is everywhere in Kazakhstan, but with an underdeveloped tourist infrastructure, the onus is on you to find it.

Ascension Cathedral (also known as Zenkov Cathedral), Panfilov Park, Medeu

Open: daily, 8am–7pm.
Services: 8am and 5pm Mon–Sat and 7am, 9am and 5pm on Sundays

This pastel-coloured wooden cathedral was designed by the Russian architect Zenkov during the Tsarist administration of Central Asia in 1904, and is one of very few buildings that survived a large earthquake in Almaty in 1911. The cathedral is situated at the centre of Panfilov Park, its domes just visible above the treetops. Said to be built without the use of a single nail,

the cathedral was used as a cultural centre and museum during Soviet times although it opened again as an Orthodox cathedral following Independence. Step inside and you are in a world of 'old' believers wearing headscarves with brooms in hand, illuminated by the light of the stained-glass windows. Visit while there is a service and you can watch the robed, bearded priest swinging incense back and forth and chanting the liturgy in deep, resonant tones against a background of elaborate icons.

Central Mosque, 16 Pushkin Street (Mametov), Medeu

Tel: 230 1774

Situated not far from the Sayakhat bus station, and like all traditional mosques not far from the city's main bazaar, Almaty's large blue-domed Central Mosque was built with state funds and completed in 1999. If the noise of the traffic subsides for long enough, you can occasionally hear the

song of the *muezzin* floating over the breeze as you walk around the city. Services are held five times a day, although the mosque is busiest at Friday lunchtime.

Green Bazaar, Dostyk Avenue (Zhibek Zholi), Medeu
Open: 9am–6pm. Closed Mondays.

Commonly referred to by its Russian name, the Green or Zelyony Bazaar is a small piece of Central Asia right in the heart of Almaty. Walk around the food section on the ground floor and meet Tajiks, Uzbeks, Koreans and Tatars selling dried fruits and nuts, delicious organic fruit and vegetables, spices, salads and all types of meat and dairy products. Even if you don't want to buy, the Green Bazaar should be on your to-do list. Two of the four columns in the main

105

food hall also serve as cafés, the perfect vantage point to drink green tea and watch people trading below you. If you are hungry, look for one of our favourite cafés in Almaty, which can be found downstairs to the left of the fruit and vegetables. Run by Uighurs, the café serves the best *laghman* (noodles with fried vegetables) we've tried in the whole town. We highly recommend it. Outside the more formally arranged food section you will find stalls selling everything from Kazakh tracksuits to Russian porcelain and essential household tools you never knew you needed.

Kazan Cathedral, 45a Haliyulina Street, Medeu
Open: daily, 8am–5pm
Services: 9am and 4pm on Sundays

This pretty, pale blue church is on the road heading east out of the city. Built in 1898, the cathedral is named in honour of the Miraculous Icon of the

Holy Mother of God of Kazan, one of Russia's most famous icons, whose feast day is celebrated at the cathedral every year on 4 November.

Kensai Graveyard, Sarsenbaev Street, east of the Zoo, Medeu

Follow Bogenbai Batyr east past the zoo and take the second right after the road doglegs to the left. Then follow the road as it climbs up the hill to the Kensai Graveyard, which you will see from the bottom. This graveyard is a fascinating place to walk around, not only because of the beautiful view of the mountains and the wooded district in which the graveyard is found, but also because of the graves themselves. Kensai houses many of Almaty's dead elite. Of particular interest are the Soviet gravestones with picture-perfect

images of the deceased engraved onto the headstones. It's interesting to see, too, quite how many Kazakhs had sayings from the Koran engraved in Arabic on their headstones at a time when atheism was state enforced.

Panfilov Park, intersected by Dostyk Avenue and Aiteke Bi St, Medeu

This rectangular park in downtown Almaty, laid out during the establishment of the original town of Verniy in the late 19th century, is one of the most pleasant areas in the city to take a stroll and people watch. In the centre of the park is a gigantic monument to the 28 Central Asian infantry soldiers

under General Panfilov who gave their lives defending the walls of Moscow (represented by the stone crenellations) from Nazi tanks in 1941. At the base of the memorial are the words of one of the 28 soldiers, V Klochkov: 'Great Russia. Beyond Moscow there is nowhere to retreat', alluding to the fact that if Moscow is lost, so is all of Russia. All 28, including Panfilov himself, were posthumously awarded the title of Hero of the Soviet Union, and you can see each of their names on separate memorial stones in the park. The monument is one of three commemorating those who were lost in battle in defence of the USSR. The three monuments are united by an eternal flame, which becomes the focal point of commemoration on 9 May (Victory Day). At weekends the monument becomes a focal point for newly-weds who arrive in cavalcades of white limousines to have their photos taken in front of the eternal flame. To the west of the memorial lies the Ascension Cathedral.

St Nicholas Cathedral, Baitursunyly St (Kabanbai Batyr), Almaly

Open: daily, 8am–7pm
Services: 9am and 5pm daily with an additional service at 7am on Sundays

Built in 1908, this golden-domed turquoise cathedral was one of two churches that held services in Almaty during late Communist times. Prior to that, it was used as a stable for the Bolshevik cavalry. Presided over by Father Valerii, the cathedral exudes a rare calm in this frenetic and fast-changing city. At Easter and Christmas you can even witness the sight of a church with bouncers, as strongmen stand at the top of the steps to keep the crowds under control.

MUSEUMS

The A. Kasteyev State Museum of Arts, 30a Satpaev St (Baizakov), Bostandyk

Tel: 247 8249

Open: 10am–6pm. Closed Mondays and the last day of the month

Entrance: 100 tenge

Located next to the National Bank and diagonally opposite the Hyatt Hotel, the Kasteyev State Museum of Arts is one of Almaty's highlights. The museum displays a wide selection of Kazakh applied art, contemporary sculpture and Russian and Western European art. Of particular interest is the museum's broad collection of Kazakh and Soviet art from the 1930s onwards.

Named after one of Kazakhstan's best known artists during the Soviet period, the Kasteyev takes you through various eras of Soviet art, as well as presenting artists, such as Sergei Kalymkov, whose philosophical musings on canvas were well ahead of, and most unusual for, his time. Other artists of note from this period displayed in the museum include Falk, Tansykbayev, Shardenov and Kenbayev. The Kasteyev has information and guides available in English and a very knowledgeable curatorial team who are kept busy rotating the display, acquiring new works and mounting diverse exhibitions. On the ground floor there are two carpets and one that sells a few paintings and antiques.

Central State Museum , 44 Furmanov Street, above Republican Square, Medeu

Open: 9.30am–6pm. Closed Tuesdays.

Price: 100 tenge

This museum offers a wide grounding in the paleontology, archaeology, geology, ethnography, natural history and pre-history of Kazakhstan, as well as

the culture of a number of the ethnicities which Kazakhstan boasts. The full-sized yurt, weapons and traditional costumes in the ethnography room are particularly interesting. For a further 1,300 tenge you can see an exhibition of Scythian gold from the *kurgans* or burial tombs of Kazakhstan.

The Geological Museum of the Republic of Kazakhstan, 85 Dostyk Avenue, Medeu

Tel: 261 5283

Open: 10am–5pm Mon–Fri

Descend down a mock mineshaft into the dazzling world of Kazakhstan's minerals. Said to have every element in Mendeleyev's periodic table within its territory, Kazakhstan is a mineralogical mosaic, and this museum is a fascinating insight into the wealth that lies beneath the expansive steppe.

Soros Centre for Contemporary Art, Block B, Sector 110, Alem 2, Dostyk Avenue, Medeu

Tel: 320 1203 or 320 1204   www.scca.kz
Open: 9am–6pm Mon–Fri

The mission of the Soros Centre for Contemporary Art, run by the energetic and intellectual Valeria Ibraeva, is the development of contemporary art in Central Asia. By holding exhibitions, seminars and workshops as well as an impressive collection of catalogues, magazines, journals and actual works by local artists, the centre aims to provide information, links and inspiration for artists living within Central Asia, and represent those artists abroad. If you are interested in learning anything about contemporary art in Central Asia, this should be your first stop. Please note, however, that difficulties with funding may mean the centre will move in early 2008, so check the website for current contact details if you plan to visit.

CONCERT HALLS

Abai Opera and Ballet Theatre, 110 Kabanbai Batyr (Panfilov), Almaly

Tel: 272 7934

The Abai Opera and Ballet Theatre is housed in a beautiful classical Soviet building designed by the Soviet architect Baisenov prior to World War II. During the war, many Russian and Soviet officers were sent to Almaty for treatment, where they were kept entertained by a programme of ongoing performances at the Opera House. At present, the season begins in September and runs through June during which time it plays host to a large number of well-known operas and ballets in repertoire, meaning that you can see *Swan Lake*, *Aida* and *Romeo and Juliet* within a week. But it's not just internationally renowned works that are aired here; the theatrical season traditionally opens with the opera *Abai*, composed by two of Kazakhstan's great musical personalities – Akhmet Zhubanov and Latiff Khamidi. If *Abai* is on while you are in town, don't miss out – it offers perhaps the most pleasant way of learning more about Kazakhstan's national folk hero.

KazakhConcert, 83 Ablai Khan Avenue (Kazibek Bi), Almaly
Tel: 279 1426
Box Office Open: 11am–6pm Mon–Fri

Every two weeks or so during the season (September to May), you can attend classical, jazz or folk concerts at KazakhConcert with local and international performers. Booking has to be done in person at the box office just inside the entrance, and posters around the town will alert you to what is on, although these tend to be in Russian or Kazakh. Tickets cost between 2,000 and 3,000 tenge depending on the event.

Philharmonic, 35 Kaldayakov St (Tole Bi), Medeu
Tel: 291 8048
Box office open: 10am-1pm and 2pm to 6pm

Palace of the Republic, Intersection of Abai and Dostyk Avenues, Medeu
Tel: 291 4366

THEATRES

Auezov Kazakh Drama Theatre, 105 Abai Avenue, Bostandyk
Tel: 292 3307

German Drama Theatre, 64d Satpaev Street, Almaty
Tel: 246 5774

Korean State Musical Comedy Theatre, 70/1 Papanin Street
Tel: 290 9548

Lermontov Russian Drama Theatre, 43 Abai Avenue, Almaty
Tel: 262 8273

Uighur State Musical Theatre, 30a Satpaev St, Bostandyk
Tel: 272 8276

FILM

Eurasia International Film Festival
www.eurasiaiff.kz

This film festival takes place annually in the last week of September. Compiled and organized by the film critic and connoisseur Gulnara Abykayeva, the festival brings together local and international films and is an important event on the Almaty film calendar.

shop...

Fans of designer clothes will find some great labels, but at a premium compared to European prices. Wait until the summer, though, and you can pick up some good bargains when shops have sales with 50–70% off. Try Gogol Street, now a skeleton of its former haute couture self and Dostyk and Satpaeva, where most of the boutiques have moved.

Also expensive, but worth visiting, are the new Kazakh designers. For Kazakh pastiche try Balnur Assanova or Kuralai Nurdakilova. Alternatively, for a trendy ready-to-wear collection, we recommend Aida Kaumenova. You can also find her clothes at Sadu's Concept Store on Al Farabi, a wonderful place to shop and drop, if you feel like a bit of lunch at the same time.

If you can't afford the high prices, you can buy designer ripoffs by the vanful at Edem, a giant superstore just before the huge Barakholka market on the out-skirts of town. The Barakholka itself is a great place to go (stick to the left-hand side of the street) for vibrant Kyrgyz tin trunks, felt carpets (*shirdaks*) and other handicrafts.

By far the best, and most convenient place for handicrafts and antique Kazakh jewellery, however, is the top floor of Tsum (Tsentralny Universalny Magazin) – the Central State Store. The many stalls on this floor offer everything from felt slippers to silk scarves, wolf skins to painted nomadic warrior chessboards.

Three times a year, there is a giant crafts fair held at the Schoolchildren's Palace on Dostyk which brings together crafts people from all across Central Asia – if you are in town when this on, don't miss the opportunity to visit it. On the last weekend of the month at the Zhetisu Hotel across the road from Tsum on Ablai Khan there is a smaller crafts fair, which is worth visiting if you are nearby.

If you have the energy, visit the flea market held on Saturdays and Sundays just beyond the city centre on the road to Chilik. It is not that easy to find, but it depends quite how dedicated a bargain hunter you are. Expect to find lots of *babushkas* with all of their possessions laid out in front of them. They will probably charge you far too little, so it's not a good idea to bargain too much.

For art, both contemporary and Soviet, there are some great galleries – the best being Tengri Umai just off the Arbat near Tsum and Elisaveta Malinovskaya's ARK Gallery in the Dostar Building on Dostyk.

Finally, don't forget the Zelyonni or Green Bazaar for dried fruits, nuts, honey, honeycomb and caviar.

ANTIQUES

Azat Akimbek Antiques, 531 Seifullin Avenue, 7th floor, Office 713 (Kazybek Bi), Almaly
Tel: 272 0806; mobile: 8 701 733 9969 or 8 333 397 6446
Open: daily, 11am–6pm

Azat Akimbek, or 'Prince' Azat Akimbek as he prefers to be known, is Almaty's premier antiques dealer – a self-styled Uighur prince from the neighbouring Xinjiang province in China. Although his prices have increased in line with the oil boom, he still has one of the best stocks in town, ranging from 19th century Russian paintings and sculpture to Soviet socialist realist art, antique Central Asian jewellery, medals and weaponry, and Russian icons. His shop is located on the seventh floor of the eight-floor Sary Arka building, but it's worth ringing ahead to make sure he's there.

Antika, 165 Furmanov St (Kurmangazy), Almaly
Tel: 267 0736
Open: 10am–6pm. Closed Sundays.

Antika offers a good collection of Soviet memorabilia, paintings, jewellery and other antiques.

ART GALLERIES

Alma-Ata Art Centre, Toyota Centre, 151 Suyunbai (Bayanulskaya), Turksib
Tel: 278 7123
Open: 10am–6pm Tues–Sat

Ark Gallery, Dostar Business Centre, 240 Dostyk Avenue (Kazhymukan), Medeu
Open: daily, 10am–6pm

Run by the phenomenally well-informed Elisaveta Malinovskaya, Ark Gallery spreads itself out over several floors of the Dostar Business Centre on

Dostyk and exhibits current Central Asian and Russian artists such as Lui-Ko and Utkin.

Oyu, Hyatt Regency Hotel, 29/6 Satpaev St, Bostandyk
Tel: 250 9791 www.oyu.kz
Open: 11am–7pm. Closed Sundays.

Part of the buildings which make up the Hyatt Hotel complex, Oyu is especially interesting for its collection of Central Asian art from the 1940s and 50s. Boasting work by artists such as Shardenov, Kasteyev, Ismailova and Sidorkin, Oyu is well worth visiting if you are serious about collecting Soviet art and conveniently located just across the road from the Kasteyev State Museum of Arts.

Tengri Umai, 103 Panfilov St, Almaly
Tel: 258 1152 or 273 5766 www.tu.kz
Open: 10am–6pm. Closed Sundays.

Director Vladimir Filatov is a well-respected gallery owner who has recently re-opened his 15-year-old gallery in a new venue. A keen patron of modern and contemporary art, he tends to keep one step ahead of his peers with excellent monthly exhibitions of Kazakh and Central Asian art. To find the gallery, go to the corner of Zhibek and Baisetov streets, walk roughly 20 metres south (uphill) on Baisetov and turn left into the courtyard. Tengri Umai is in the multi-storeyed building straight in front of you and the door is round to the left.

Ular Art Gallery, Academy of Sciences, 29 Kurmangazy St (Valikhanov), Medeu
Tel: 272 4783
Open: daily, 10am–7pm

CARPETS

Buying carpets in Almaty isn't quite the same experience as it is in places like Istanbul where you might sit for hours in the bazaar drinking tea with the shop owner and negotiating prices back and forth. In Almaty, you won't find much in terms of traditional crafts in the bazaars. Rather, carpet shopping is a more straightforward transaction with a few shops set up around the city. We've listed the ones we recommend below.

Bukhara Carpets, Office 103, 103 Furmanov St (Aiteke Bi), Almaly
Tel: 267 0510 www.bukhara-carpets.com
Open: daily, 9am–6pm

By far the most extensive selection of Kazakh, Turkmen, Afghan, Caucasian, Chinese and Persian carpets in Almaty, Bukhara Carpets is sure to have something for your liking. The knowledgeable proprietors, Akul Nakov and Dmitriy Smolenskiy, can help you find just what you're looking for, and also have a selection of tent bands, *suzannis* and other textiles from around Central Asia. Their website has an updated listing of their stock and other textile-related information.

Carpet Shop, 187b Furmanov St (Abai), Central Almaty
Tel: 272 2245; mobile: 8 701 771 0723
Open: daily, 10am–7pm

Amunalla Shaffie sells a selection of antique and modern carpets from Central Asia, Afghanistan and the Caucasus. There is generally a sign outside pointing to his shop, which is in the Soviet-looking building just next to Line Brew (see Drink). It's best to ring first to make sure the shop is open.

Mr Muhammad's Carpet Museum, 92 Panfilov St (Aiteke Bi), Almaly
Mobile: 8 701 334 4036
Open: daily, 10am–5pm

Mr Muhammad's carpet shop is just down from Bukhara Carpets. The entrance to this tiny shop is actually on Aiteke Bi between Furmanov and

Panfilov streets, and there's usually a small sign sitting on the Furmanov side pointing to it.

CHOCOLATE, VODKA AND COGNAC

> ### Rahat Chocolate Factory and Store, Zhibek Zholi St (Kaldayakov), Medeu
> Tel: 230 2258
> Open: daily, 8am–8pm

You won't need a map to find the Rahat Chocolate Factory; just sniff your way towards the delicious chocolate scented air wafting from the eastern edge of the Green Bazaar. This chocolate factory is an institution in Almaty dating back to Soviet times when school children used to go for sweet-smelling tours inside. Privatized by the President's son-in-law (whose name the factory bears), Rahat is still churning out chocolate delights today. You can find Rahat chocolates all over Almaty (and Kazakhstan for that matter); individually wrapped chocolates are sold by the kilo from clear containers in just about every kiosk and shop around. More fun, though, is to buy directly from the source where you can take away chocolate bars with names such as Kazakhstan, Almaty, Astana, Alatau, Atyrau, Tomiris and Sary Arka (Golden Steppe) that are emblazoned with images of the Golden Man, Koktubey, the Hotel Kazakhstan, Baiterek and more.

Vodka and cognac

Vodka and cognac are two of the most plentiful domestic products Kazakhstan has to offer, and always a fun present to bring back from the steppe. From the omnipresent street kiosk to any grocery store, you'll find shelves stocked full with more varieties of both spirits than even a hedonist could ever imagine. The names are about as varied as the selection and, much like the chocolate, have a resounding sense of nationalism. Some fun vodka names to look for are: Khan, Admiral, Black Gold, Berkut (Kazakh for golden eagle), Astana, and Moscow. For cognac, you'll find Nomad, Ak Orda, Al-Farabi, Khan Tengri, Turkestan, Sary Arka and, of course, Tamerlane.

The most fashionable vodka to come to town, though, is Snow Queen. Currently served in some of the hippest bars in New York, Washington, Moscow, London and Paris, Snow Queen is a favourite among the likes of Mick Jagger, P. Diddy and Scarlett Johannson. Given Kazakhstan's plentiful organic wheat production and cold mountain water, it's an ideal location for premium vodka production. Snow Queen can be found in most food shops around Almaty; just look out for its chic frosted bottle. If you prefer trying it first, have a few ice-cold shots at Crystal (see Party).

CRAFTS

Assia, 85 Kazybek Bi St (Tchaikovskovo), Almaly
Tel: 278 0632
Open: 11am–7pm (6pm Sat). Closed Sundays.

Run by Aizhan, the wife of Russian film director, Sergei Bodrov, Assia is a small crafts shop with a wide selection of carpets from throughout Central Asia plus ceramics, textiles, paintings, jewellery, antique *chapans* (Central Asian robes) from Uzbekistan and Turkmenistan, local materials, *suzannis* and *tuz kiz* (Uzbek and Kazakh embroideries). Three times a year (in March, May and December), Aizhan helps organize large craft fairs at the Schoolchildren's Palace on Dostyk that bring together artisans from all over Central Asia. For more information, ring or email Aizhan on b_aizhan@gmail.ru or b_aizhan@ok.kz.

CAMP Bazaar, 40 Orbita 1, Bostandyk
Tel: 255 0442 www.campkazakhstan.org

With a shop situated in their office in the Orbita Mikrorayon, CAMP Bazaar is not easy to find. The easiest way is to take a taxi along Al-Farabi Avenue, turn right into Mustafin Street and turn right opposite the Baikonur Cinema. Then take the first left, and first right and keep going into a large green yard. CAMP Bazaar's office is in the large two-floor Soviet building to the right. It may be difficult to find (and it is worth phoning if you are having difficulties), but the hunt is worth it. CAMP stands for Central Asia Mountain Partnership, and the beautiful felt and silk objects you find here are part of a larger programme of sustainable development that includes cheese making, wicker furniture and more. The organization works with repatriated Kazakhs from Mongolia and Xinjiang province in China who have returned to Almaty to work, and who have retained skills that many native Kazakhs have lost. When looking at the prices, bear in mind that one of their exquisitely woven silk and felt scarves can take six days to make. If you have the time and the ideas, CAMP Bazaar is happy to take commissions too.

Hotel Zhetisu Crafts Fair, 55 Ablai Khan Avenue (Makataev), Zhetisu
Tel: 250 0400

A crafts fair is held in the lobby of the Hotel Zhetisu on the last weekend of every month with a selection of carpets, crafts and traditional goods on display. With many vendors coming up from Uzbekistan to flaunt their wares, it's well worth a visit if you happen to be in town.

Tsum, Corner of Ablai Khan Avenue (Zhibek Zholi), Zhetisu
Open: daily, 10am–9pm (8pm Sun)

The top floor of this central department store is a treasure trove of small stores selling felt slippers, toys, bags, dolls, mini yurts, decorative chessboards with Mongol warriors, cushion covers made from old Kazakh embroideries, traditional and modern Kazakh jewellery, hats, coats and more. If you are looking for presents to take home, this is the place to go.

DESIGNER CLOTHING

Designer clothes have hit Almaty – and in a big way. Just about all high-end labels can be found in this most fashionable city, and although you won't find many bargains as prices are often much higher than on Madison Avenue, it's still fun to window-shop. The block of Gogol Street between Furmanov and Ablai Khan used to be Almaty's fashion district until it migrated farther south to Satpaev. Gogol is worth a look, though, as there are still some shops there – Armani is the most recent addition.

Almaty's newest fashion centre is on Satpaev Street in the Business District. The block between Furmanov and Dostyk is full of shops that could leave you penniless, such as Strenesse, L'Occitane and Sauvage Home Collection. Word has it that even Manolo Blahnik is opening up here in early 2008. Three of our favourites are:

Bureau 1985, 116 Dostyk Avenue (Satpaev), Medeu
Tel: 262 9003
Open: 11am–8pm. Closed Sundays.

Situated on the ground floor of the large Sergio Interiors showroom at the corner of Dostyk and Satpaev, this small boutique is simply the best place in Almaty to find cutting-edge designers, such as Martin Margiela, Yohji Yamamoto and Dries van Noten. The entrance to the store is on Satpaev Street.

Sauvage Boutique, 4a Satpaev St (Dostyk), Medeu
Tel: 264 4369 or 263 1190
Open: daily, 10.30am–8pm

Sauvage is a fashionable delight, with collections for men and women by Donna Karan, Alexander McQueen, Stella McCartney, Burberry, Tod's, Balenciaga, Marc Jacobs, John Galliano, Prada and Chloe (just to name a few) you'll be hard pressed not to fall in love with something on Sauvage's racks. Sauvage is the product of Almaty's most fashion-conscious proprietor who represents over 300 European brands in Kazakhstan and has a variety of other boutiques around town, like Rush (featuring Comme des Garcons, Miu Miu, Paul Smith and Etro) near Posh Bar (see Drink), Pro Mode (with over 30 different brands of jeans) next to Ramstore, and Baby Dior on Gogol. The staff at Sauvage can point you in the direction of these. Keep your eyes peeled as Sauvage will be opening a new 1,800-square-metre fashion boutique on Timiryazev and Seifullin. We don't know the name yet, but the store will introduce even more brands for Almaty's fashionistas and will be located near the new JW Marriott Esentai Hotel (see Sleep), which is set to become another shopping haven. Look out, too, for a fashion café to open near the Zhailjau Golf Resort sometime in 2008.

Top Line and Top Secret, 244 Furmanov St (Al-Farabi), Medeu
Tel: 265 1087
Open: daily, 11am–8pm

Where do Almaty's hedonists go for their Jimmy Choo's and Christian Louboutin heels? Top Line, of course. With the best selection, by far, of designer shoes, Top Line will sort out all your footwear needs. You'll find it directly across the street from Palladium's Piano Bar (see Eat). Also, don't miss Top Secret, next door to Top Line, for designer lingerie. We're sure La Perla's latest will complement those new high heels…

FUR

Meha, 151 Panfilov St (Kurmangazy), Almaly
Open: daily, 10am–6pm

Meha, which translates as fur, offers a wide selection of fur coats, hats, jackets, belts and more from Turkey.

Royal Furs, 92 Ablai Khan Avenue (Kabanbai Batyr), Almaly
Tel: 237 8665 or 237 8666
Open: daily, 10am–7pm

You might walk out of Royal Furs a pauper, but you will definitely be a princess. All the best Italian furs are available here including labels such as Gianfranco Ferre and Braschi. Choose from a selection of coats, jackets, hats, stoles, belts, bags, scarves and even a fur dressing gown.

JEWELLERY

Zerger Ilyas 'Diamond World' Gallery, 177/1 Furmanov St (Abai), Almaly
Tel: 267 0901
Open: 11am–7pm (6pm Sat). Closed Sundays.

Inspired by the ancient tribes who roamed the Kazakh steppe, Ilyas Suleimenov and his team of designers have been making exquisite modern jewellery since 1991. Better known in Paris, Zurich and Moscow, Ilyas's jewellery is now becoming popular with the Kazakh elite. If you want to treat yourself to pure indulgence, pop into his studio and try on a diamond- and ruby-studded tiara with a giant aquamarine at its centre inspired by the ancient local queen of the Massagetae tribe, Tomiris, or as we know her, the queen of the Amazons.

KAZAKH DESIGNERS

Almaty's high-class fashion boom is complemented by a number of top-notch local designers that are well worth checking out if you're in the mood for something more unique.

Aida Kaumenova at the Sadu Concept Store, Mercur Town, Samal 3/25 (Furmanov), Medeu
Tel: 271 6865
Open: daily, noon–midnight

Aida Kaumenova is the first of the Kazakh designers to introduce a prêt-a-porter collection. Her cutting-edge fashion line, Aida KaumeNOVA, is largely inspired by fashion guru Vivienne Westwood, and is available for sale in the Sadu Concept Store (see Eat).

AK Studio, 78 Kabanbai Batyr (Pushkin), Medeu
Tel: 291 3861
Open: 10am–7pm (5pm Sat). Closed Sundays.

AK Studio features designer Aigul Kassymova's styles that blend a bit of traditional Kazah with a modern twist. Her trademark is a large, red Almaty apple, and she has some hip-looking T-shirts for sale that stylishly emblazon the Golden Man (and the apple) on the front – definitely something you won't find at home!

Kuralai Couture, 112 Zheltoksan Street (corner of Kazybek Bi), Almaly

Tel: 279 6767 www.kuralai-n.kz

Open: 10am–7pm (5pm Sat). Closed Sundays.

Designer Kuralai Nurkadilova takes her inspiration from John Galliano, and combines vibrant colours and crystals with traditional Kazakh designs to create some shocking pieces of Kazakh haute couture. With boutiques in Paris, Moscow, Astana, Atyrau, Aktau, Shimkent and Almaty, don't miss your chance to check out this unique seamstress.

The VIP Fashion Salon of Symbat Fashion Academy, 43 Kunaev St (Zhibek Zholi), Medeu

Tel: 273 3469 or 258 2313 www.symbat.kz

Open: 10am–7pm. Closed Sundays.

Balnur Assanova is the head designer for Symbat Fashion Academy, Central Asia's leading fashion house. Drawing inspiration from Kazakh national designs, Assanova mixes hand embroidery, beads and semi-precious stones to create her stunning modern masterpieces.

MARKETS

Barakholka, on the road to Ainabulak

Open: 8am–5pm. Closed Mondays.

This is a behemoth of a bazaar on the outskirts of town that actually consists of a number of different bazaars, each with its own name. To get there, head west on Raimbek Avenue and then take a right when you get to Rozybakiev Street and keep going until you know you're there (it's pretty obvious). The bazaar is stuffed full of cheap designer rip-offs from neighbouring China, car parts, dishes, household supplies, live animals and a muddled mass of so much more. If you look hard through the rabbit warren of stalls positioned on the left-hand side of the road, you will also find traditional goods such as painted tin trunks from Kyrgyzstan, felt slippers, toys, Christmas tree decorations, enamel teapots, Russian woollen scarves, *dombras* (traditional Kazakh two-stringed instruments), Kazakh national costumes, and much, much more. On the right-hand side at Alatau I Bazaar, you'll find fur coats and hats, and right at the beginning of the market you'll find Adem and Al Farabi – two enormous covered markets with high(er)-quality goods from China which are well worth a visit for the shop-a-holics among you. The Barakholka is one of the busiest spots in Almaty (and one that requires a lot of energy), but it's a great juxtaposition of local flare set against Almaty's more cosmopolitan centre.

Green Bazaar, Intersection of Zhibek Zholi Street and Dostyk Avenue
Open: 9am–6pm. Closed Mondays.

Head for the central building in Almaty's Green (Zelyony) Bazaar if you want to buy dried fruit and nuts from Uzbekistan and Tajikistan, locally-produced honey and honeycomb, herbs, spices, dried flower and herbal teas, Caspian caviar, and even aloe vera juice for those who need a thorough cleansing. In the adjoining rows outside, you'll also find items such as fishnet stockings at a quarter of what they would cost in the UK and ribbon at a fraction of what you might pay in VV Rouleaux. A small, informal flea market sets up shop at the end of Dostyk Avenue just before the Green Bazaar. While not always there, if it is set up, it's a great place to find old Soviet pins, ceramics, jewellery, books and more.

Flea Market, on the road towards Chilik
Open: Saturday and Sunday mornings

Located at the back of the Otau Bazaar, which you'll find on the right side of the road just after turning left to Chilik at the large roundabout on Haliullin Street, the flea market or 'Totalisator' is a great place to find old Soviet memorabilia and goods. The ultimate in recycling, this is where Almaty's *babushkas* come to sell what often seems like a lifetime of personal possessions, so be generous.

MALLS

In the event that you need to do some basic shopping for a few essentials, go to Mega Alma-Ata or Ramstore. From clothing boutiques, to supermarkets, food-courts, cinemas and even an ice-skating rink, they should have everything you could ever need.

Mega Center Alma-Ata, 247 Rozybakiev St (Al-Farabi), Bostandyk

Opened in winter 2006, Mega is the newest mall to hit Almaty it also has branches in Astana and Shimkent.

Ramstore Hypermarket, Furmanov St (Zholdasbekov), Medeu

Ramstore (which looks like PAMCTOP in Russian) is the largest supermarket chain in Turkey, and is known by all taxi drivers in Almaty. There are a few locations in Almaty, but this is the original and the best. Just look for the giant, green kangaroo outside, and you'll know you have arrived.

MUSEUM SHOPS

Central State Museum, 44 Furmanov St (Republican Square), Medeu
Open: 9.30am–6pm. Closed Tuesdays.

There are three shops inside the museum's lobby selling a variety of antique carpets as well as other Central Asian textiles and handicrafts. The shop with the best selection is up the steps and straight ahead.

The A. Kasteyev State Museum of Arts, 30a Satpaev St (Baizakov), Bostandyk
Open: 10am–6pm. Closed Mondays and the last day of the month.

Two stores in the Kasteyev Museum offer a good selection of Central Asian carpets. A small shop selling Kazakh paintings, antiques and traditional jewellery is also worth a look.

play...

Suffering from a hangover and too much food? There are a number of ways to relax in Almaty, both within and outside the city limits.

If you really want to freshen up, the place to go is the Central Public Baths, or Arasan Banya. A two-hour session there is good value and thoroughly invigorating. If you prefer to be pampered, try the Bali Spa at the Grand Tien Shan Hotel where you can get a Balinese massage or relax in their marble *hammam*. For a more indulgent experience, try the Luxor Wellness Club, housed in an Egyptian-style building on the way up to Medeo.

Another place to spot the Almaty elite is Zhailjau Golf Resort (below), an Arnold Palmer-designed course on the southwestern outskirts of the city with breathtaking panoramic views of the mountains. For a more down to earth golfing experience, try the more established Nurtau Golf Club, adjacent to the Alatau Sanatorium.

If you're feeling active, the place to head in both summer and winter is to Medeo and beyond. Just 20 minutes out of the city centre, Medeo is a wonderful starting point for numerous hikes into the Zhailiskii Alatau Mountains. In the winter, the giant outdoor skating rink comes alive at night and is a great way to

spend your evening. Another eight kilometres or so further up the road is Chimbulak, Kazakhstan's best ski resort. Currently being developed, you can still ski or snowboard on its four main slopes, snow providing, and it's possible to hire all equipment up there. In addition to skiing, skating and snowboarding, there's plenty to do in the mountains for the extreme sports lover: think mountain climbing, mountain biking, hot air ballooning, quad biking – almost anything is possible at a price.

If you prefer water to the mountains, head to Lake Kapchagai just 60 kilometres northeast of Almaty; in the summer you can hire out a 35 foot French sail-

ing yacht – the ultimate get away from the hustle, bustle and smog of city life. For a more adventurous weekend away, it is also possible to do some big game fishing on the Ili River delta. While it will set you back considerably, think of the tall stories you can tell.

If you have a day or two to spare, and feel like an expedition, you'll find there are lots of day excursions outside the city. You can visit a small orthodox monastery in a valley to the west of Almaty or gaze at images of Buddha engraved into rocks close to the Ili river, followed by having a picnic on the riverbank. If you happen to be in the region in May or June, a trip into the steppe to see the wildflowers, which cover it at that time of year, is a must. You can drive to local lakes, go horse riding and stay in yurts. For excursions of this sort, though, it is worth booking in advance. Tourism is very much in the developmental stages here, and sometimes the simplest things take time to find.

EXCURSIONS AROUND ALMATY

One of Almaty's most attractive points is the easy access to the wide range of natural attractions on its doorstep. Not every city has mountains of 4,000 metres or more on one side and an endless steppe on the other. So if you have the time to take an excursion for a day or two, we highly recommend it. Below is a list of activities around the city ranging from one- to three- day excursions. If you need help organizing any of these trips, just contact one of the travel agents listed at the end.

Aksai Gorge

Twenty kilometres to the west of Almaty in the Aksai Gorge, a small Russian Orthodox Monastery has been built on the site of a former monastery destroyed by the Bolsheviks in the early years of the Soviet Union. If you're prepared for a short hike, it's possible to visit the two monks living here, who built the wooden monastery in memory of the martyred priests Seraphim and Feognost. The Ecotourism Information Resource Centre can help you to get there.

Altyn Emel National Park

This national park, just to the northeast of Lake Kapchagai, covers 90 square kilometres between the Ili River and the Ak Tau mountain range. A habitat for a rich variety of wildlife including steppe antelope, the park is best known for the beautiful Singing Sand Dunes (some of which are 80 metres high) that lie at the eastern end of the park and hum in the wind. In addition, there are ancient Scythian burial mounds (Scythians were nomadic tribes who populated the Kazakh steppe between the 8th and 2nd centuries BC) and Bronze Age petroglyphs in some of the valleys within the park.

Big Almaty Lake

Set in a valley high above Almaty in the Ili-Alatau National Park in Alma Arasan Gorge, is the vivid turquoise Big Almaty Lake at 2,510 metres. 1.5km long and 35m deep, the alpine lake is a destination in itself, or a good start to one of the many hikes in the area. Situated a few kilometres before the lake is Alpine Rose, a hotel run by Alpina XXI (see Mountain Retreats), and just beyond the lake is the Tien Shan Astronomical Observatory where you can watch the stars through the Observatory's telescope.

Charyn Canyon

This magnificent 300-metre deep canyon is located approximately 200km east of Almaty. The main canyon runs along the Charyn River with parched red rocks that are somewhat reminiscent of the Grand Canyon. Best visited in April/May or September/October, time your visit to reach the canyon by early evening as the light on the rock formations is unimaginably beautiful. Because the canyon is quite a drive from Almaty, camping facilities are also available.

Eagle Hunting

Surely the purest form of hunting there is, nothing quite beats a weekend in the countryside with an eagle on your arm. Falconry is an ancient tradition in this formerly nomadic country with some practitioners dating it back to the Scythians. While the origins are obscure there is no doubt that the Kazakh nomads who populated these lands from the 15th century onwards have a unique tradition of hunting with golden eagles. The hunting season begins in November and is over by the middle of February. Usually pursued on horseback, the prey includes foxes, hares, rabbits and small mountain antelopes. Both Jibek Joly and Silk Road Adventures are able to organize a trip, but beware it doesn't come cheap.

Ili River

Take a trip to the Ili River to see rock drawings of Buddha at Tamgaly Tas and stay for a picnic along the riverbank. Or why not arrange a trip up the river by boat, and if you're there between April and June, make sure to stop in the steppe and see the wild tulips and poppies that blanket the area.

Kol Say Lakes

Situated a four- to five-hour drive from Almaty, the three Kol Say lakes are absolutely exquisite and well worth a weekend visit – or longer if you have the time. Despite Kazakhstan's lengthy equine heritage this is one of only a few places that offers organized horse trekking. The tour company Jibek Joly has a guesthouse on the shores of the first lake, with its own *banya*, or if you prefer, during summer, you can stay in a yurt.

Tamgaly

The archaeological site of Tamgaly roughly three hours from Almaty in the Chu-Ili mountains (not to be confused with Tamgaly Tas by the Ili river) has a collection of some 5,000 petroglyphs (rock drawings) dating from the second half of the second millennium BC right up to the beginning of the 20th century depicting nomadic steppe life and murals illustrating traditional rituals. This dense concentration of petroglyphs is considered so important that UNESCO made it a World Heritage site in 2004. The Tamgaly gorge also contains burial sites and *kurgans* (burial mounds) from the Bronze Age and Iron Age respectively.

Turgen Gorge

The Turgen Gorge in the Ili-Alatau National Park is home to seven waterfalls, and is a wonderful place for day hikes and mountain biking. The Medvezhny (bear) Falls drop 30 metres between overhanging cliffs and fir trees, and the Bozgul Falls are so ferocious they have worn a tunnel into the rock. About 15km before reaching the gorge, you arrive at Stetson Rancho. Run by the Stetson Bar in Almaty, the ranch has 28 pleasant rooms that cost from 25,000–40,000 tenge. If you stay at the ranch, staff will organise picnics to the waterfalls and short riding trips if you wish. The ranch also has a swimming pool, sauna, billiards room, cinema and restaurant. For reservations, contact the main office at Stetson Bar: 128 Furmanov Street (corner of Kabanbai Batyr), tel: 261 2501 (www.stetson.kz).

The following travel agents are able to help arrange any of the above excursions. They can also arrange longer trips should you have the time or inclination.

Central Asia Tourism Company (CAT), 20 Kazybek Bi St (Kaldayakov), Medeu

Tel: 250 1070 www.centralasiatourism.com

This is Kazakhstan's most established tour agency – expensive but very efficient.

Ecotourism Information Resource Centre, 71 Zheltoksan St (Gogol), Almaly
Tel: 278 0289   www.ecotourism.kz

Set up in 2005, the Ecotourism Information Resource Centre is a noble initiative that works to promote community-based tourism. Although outside funding for the centre has recently come to an end, the centre hopes to keep going, although it may be taken over by the Kazakhstan Tourist Association. They can help organize most of the excursions above, although the emphasis is on getting there on your own (with their valuable background information on how to do so, of course).

Jibek Joly, 55 Ablai Khan Avenue, Almaly
Tel: 250 0444   www.jibekjoly.kz

Jibek Joly is well versed in organizing excursions and even runs their own guesthouses in various parts of Almaty Oblast, including at Kol Say Lakes.

Max Travel, Office 210, 10 Abai Avenue, Bostandyk
Tel: 272 5070   www.maxtravel.kz

New, highly enthusiastic, and dedicated solely to inbound tourism, Max Travel can organise a wide variety of excursions around Almaty as well as further afield to some of Kazakhstan's less-explored destinations. The photos on their website are worth the visit alone.

Silk Road Adventures, 117/44 Adi Sharipova St, Bostandyk
Tel: 292 6319 or 292 4042   www.silkroadadventures.net

Stan Tours
Tel: +7 705 118 4619 (David Berghoff)   www.stantours.com

David Berghoff has been running Stan Tours from Almaty for years and is a tremendous source of information for any tourism-related query. He specializes in trips to Turkmenistan, but is able to organize almost anything around Almaty.

EXTREME SPORTS

A number of agencies and clubs in and around Almaty offer the opportunity to participate in extreme (and sometimes less extreme) sports.

Extremal, 99b Dostyk Avenue (Al-Farabi), Medeu
Tel: 253 1499 www.extremal.kz
Open: daily, 10am–8pm

On any given day, Extremal is packed with Almaty's most extreme cyclists trading tips and making repairs. The friendly atmosphere makes it the kind of place you can pop by for some local advice – and maybe even find a cycling partner to explore beyond Almaty's traffic-jammed streets. Extremal rents out bikes, snowboards, ice-skates, skis and camping equipment. In summer, they organize bike trips to places like the Turgen waterfalls (see Excursions around Almaty), Big Almaty Lake, Charyn Canyon and even to Lake Issyk-Kul (just over the mountains in Kyrgyzstan). Snowboarding and skiing lessons are offered in winter.

Gift Idea, Office 28, 565 Seifullin Avenue, (Amangeldi), Almaly
Tel: 260 6975 www.giftidea.kz
Open: 10am–7pm Mon–Fri

Gift Idea claim they can organize anything you could ever want to do, and they mean anything (at a price). They specialize in adrenaline activities (among others) including paragliding and parachuting, hot air balloon rides, flying lessons and short trips, quad-biking in the mountains, snowmobiles, karting and helicopter rides around Almaty. As far as we can work out, if you name it, they will arrange it.

Kan Tengri, 10 Kasteyev St, Koktubey Microsdistrict, Medeu
Tel: 291 0200, 291 0880 or 291 6006 www.kantengri.kz

KanTengri are the experts in assisting with mountain climbing, heli-skiing, ski touring and other extreme sports. They also run the Karkara base camp at Khan Tengri, Kazakhstan's highest (and the Tien Shan's second highest) and most revered mountain with a 6,995-metre peak. Their president and founder is Dr Kazbek Valiyev, the first Kazakh to climb Everest and president of the Kazakhstan Mountaineering Foundation, making them a more than qualified source for all things mountaineering.

ReActive Travel Adventure, Hotel Alma-Ata, 85 Kabanbai Batyr (Panfilov), Almaly
Tel: 272 4559, 272 0002 or 272 8866   www.reactive.kz
Open: 9am–7pm Mon–Fri

If you want to go paintballing, rafting, flying, paragliding or take a trip in a hot air balloon – be proactive, ring ReActive. They can organize excursions to any of Almaty's nearby attractions (including riding trips in the Turgen Gorge), and also offer a city tour for those who wish to explore Almaty a little more deeply.

FISHING

Ili River Delta

If big game fishing is your thing, then a trip to the Ili River Delta is the ultimate experience Kazakhstan has to offer. But first things first, you will need at least four or five days and a lot of money. Once you've cleared the time and emptied your bank account, the real adventure begins. From Almaty, you travel 80km north of the petroglyphs at Tamgaly Tas on the Ili River. Then it's time to jump into a boat that will speed along the river where you can take part in some serious cat fishing among the reeds and pelicans of this immense delta. For more information, try David at Stantours, Jibek Joly or Kan Tengri, and remember to organize this trip well in advance.

GOLF

Nurtau Golf Club, Alatau Sanatorium, Upper Kamenka Village
Pro Shop: 295 8823, 295 8824 or 295 8826   www.nurtau.kz
Season: April–November (weather permitting)

Originally established in 1996 as the nine-hole Interlux Golf Club, Nurtau is now a fully fledged 18-hole golf course boasting over 250 members. The more mature of Almaty's two 18-hole clubs, Nurtau stands in the beautifully landscaped grounds of the Alatau Sanatorium and is viewed as the more democratic, or at least the cheaper, of the clubs. Golf is immensely popular in post-independence Kazakhstan thanks to the approval and interest of the President who plays off a handicap of 16. Green fees for visitors cost between 10,000 and 15,000 tenge depending on the day of the week, and clubs, shoes and other equipment are available for hire. There are a driving range and practice greens adjacent to the clubhouse. A number of tournaments take place at the club including the Kazakhstan leg of the European Challenge Tour, the Kazakhstan Open and the President's Golf Cup.

Zhailjau Golf Resort, 188 Dulaty Street (Al-Farabi), Miras District

Tel: reception 277 7621; pro shop 277 7648 www.zgr.kz
Season: April–November (weather permitting)

With its Arnold Palmer designed course, Zhailjau is designed with one thing in mind: luxury. This club proves that what the Soviets thought about golf is correct – it is a bourgeois sport. With green fees starting at 12,000 tenge on a weekday and double that at the weekend, rest assured that you will only be mixing with Almaty's crème de la crème. In addition to the beautiful setting and exquisitely designed 18-hole course, which improves year on year as the landscaping matures, Zhailjau also offers a fully stocked pro shop, a sports bar, the Dali restaurant (see Eat) and a VIP lounge (although everybody at Zhailjau seems to be a VIP) plus lessons, a driving range, putting and chipping greens, and even a spa. Be sure to finish off your day with a drink at Zhailjau's world-class clubhouse with what could be one of the most spectacular mountain-ringed views from any clubhouse in the world.

HIKING

Almaty is nestled in the foothills of the spectacular Tien Shan mountain range. Translated as 'Celestial Mountains', it would be blasphemous not to go hiking if you're planning to spend time in the city between June and September. There are more than 50 hikes around Almaty, so we recommend that you buy one of the following books, *Trekking in Russia and Central Asia* by Frith Maier or *The Hiker's Guide to Almaty* by Arkady Pozdeyev, or get in touch with one of the tour operators listed in the Excursions section if you feel you need some more personalized advice. For the best maps head to either Akademkniga (91/97 Furmanov St, tel: 273 7818) where they sell trail maps, such as 'Po Severnomy Tien Shan' (in the Northern Tien Shan) or Geo Cartographic Firm (155 Tole Bi St, room 500, 4th floor, tel: 268 4019) for more topographic, political and city maps of Kazakhstan.

MOUNTAIN RETREATS

Alpina XXI, 278-1 Dostyk Avenue, Almaly
Tel: 264 0325, 254 1648 or 260 7215   www.alpina.kz

There are two mountain hotels located not far from the city that are excellent places to stay if you're planning to hike around Almaty. Both hotels, Vorota Tuyuk Su and Alpine Rose, are run by the Almaty-based firm Alpina XXI who are extremely knowledgeable about local trails and can help organize hiking itineraries from both hotels. Vorota Tuyuk Su sits roughly 1.5km above Chimbulak. This small, rustic 26-room hotel has four wooden cottages, a billiards room, *banya* and, in the winter, snowmobiles. It is situated in the beautiful Malaya Almatinka Gorge with stunning views through the fir trees of the pyramid-shaped Mount Kumbel. From here you can also walk to the Tuyuk Su glacier (3,500 metres above sea level). The Alpine Rose Hotel is nestled 2,300 metres above sea level just below Big Almaty Lake. Its three mountain cottages, billiards room, sauna, and restaurant, reminiscent of a ski-lodge, are the perfect jumping-off spot to explore the more than 20 nearby hikes. In winter months, snowmobiles and ski equipment are also available for hire. Alpina XXI can also organize other alpinist activities as well as helicopter trips over the Tien Shan Mountains and fishing on Lake Balkhash.

RACING & RIDING

Ak Bulak Stud, Arman Territory, Talgar
Tel: 8 701 359 7799

In the small town of Talgar, to the east of Almaty, it is possible both to take riding lessons and to hack around the surrounding area. Prices start at 2,000 tenge per hour for a simple hack and 2,500 tenge an hour for riding lessons. Ring Irina Chainikova (good German and French, limited English) for information.

Altyn Tai Stud, west of the Alatau Sanatorium
Tel: 35 16 09

Call Sergei Mikhailovich, the director of this stud, to organise lessons or local hacks.

Hippodrome, 10a Omarova St, Turksib
Tel: 294 8600 www.ippodrom.kz

Almaty's hippodrome lies to the north of the city. The season begins in mid-May and lasts until mid-October with racing taking place on Sundays at roughly fortnightly intervals. It is also possible to ride at the hippodrome: ring Lyuda on 8 701 158 8745 for lessons from 2,000 tenge per hour.

Travel agents can help arrange horse trekking in Kazakhstan, but it's surprisingly hard to find given the country's equine heritage. One of the best places to go trekking is around the Kol Say Lakes to the southeast of Almaty. See our Excursions Around Almaty section for details.

SAILING

The Caspian Sea

If you really feel like blowing your inheritance, go sailing on one of two 36-foot plus catamarans on the Caspian Sea. The skipper in charge of the boats is called Andre – call him on 8 701 522 8230 to find out about afternoon and overnight jaunts to Kuryk, Bautino, the Seal Islands and Kinderley – or open sea stargazing. Prices start from $150 an hour. Okay, so the Caspian is not exactly next door to Almaty, but that's where the inheritance comes in as you will have to either fly to Aktau on Air Astana or charter your own plane. To charter a plane contact either International Jet Tour (49/61 Naurysbai Batyr, tel: 237 0631 or 237 1482, www.ijt.kz) or Skyservice (124 Al-Farabi Avenue, tel: 253 8888 or 253 8464, www.aeroplan.kz).

Lake Kapchagai
Tel: 272 5556 or 272 5566 www.7ft.kz

Almaty, thousands of miles from any sea or ocean, is not somewhere you might readily associate with sailing. Times are changing and a 35-foot French sailing yacht, *Calista,* is now permanently docked on Lake Kapchagai, 70km north of Almaty. You can hire *Calista*, her captain and one member of crew for a minimum of three hours. Sailing on the lake, an artificial body of water over 120km long and 25km wide, is perhaps one of the most pleasurable days out to be had near Almaty; the wide expanse of water with the mountains glimmering gently to the south is magical. *Calista* accomodates up to eight guests (six overnight). You can hire the boat for a weekend and head off to an island on the lake to swim in the clean water, fish and barbeque. The season runs from April to November, and it is worth calling four to five days in advance to ensure availability. Prices start from $200 an hour to hire the boat and travel to and from the lake from Almaty can be arranged.

SKATING

Medeo Outdoor Skating Rink, Malaya Almatinka Gorge
Tel: 271 6217
Open: daily, noon (10am Sat/Sun)–10pm

Medeo, which sits in the mountains just above Almaty (before you reach Chimbulak), claims to be one of the highest Olympic-sized ice stadiums in the world. It is surrounded by snow-covered pine forests, and perhaps the most pleasant time to skate is in the evening when the rink opens between noon and 10pm (otherwise the rink is open at weekends). The season lasts from November to April, cold weather permitting, and entrance costs 500 tenge. Skates can be hired from 600 tenge for two hours, but if you want good-quality skates, it is best to bring your own. Local buses to Medeo (number six which stops at the bus stop opposite the Hotel Kazakhstan) leave Almaty every 20 minutes or so until late evening and it takes around 20 minutes to climb up to Medeo. Like Chimbulak, Medeo is also undergoing reconstruction, with plans to have residential apartments, villas and a hotel designed by New York-based Robert A.M. Stern Architects open by 2010.

SKIING

Chimbulak

www.chimbulak.com

Conveniently located just 25 minutes from Almaty, Chimbulak currently boasts the best skiing facilities Kazakhstan has to offer. Often overcrowded at weekends, Chimbulak's four chairlifts and pisted slopes offer an enjoyable day out for skiers and snowboarders alike. From the Talgar Pass at 3,613m to the main lodge at 2, 260m, the resort offers a respectable vertical drop of nearly 1,000 metres with magnificent views of Almaty and the Kazakh steppe as you descend. Once back at the resort, warm up with a cup of hot chocolate and some of the best sturgeon *shashlik* in Almaty. The season at Chimbulak runs from November to April, snow provided. Good skis, boots and snowboards can be hired within the resort for about $25 a day. Renting your equipment in Almaty is somewhat cheaper. One popular shop on the way up the hill to Chimbulak is Extremal (see Extreme Sports), which also sells cross-country skis and skates. Prices start at $200 for skis and boots.

During the 2006–07 season, lifts cost 300 tenge per lift or 3,000 tenge for the day. Big changes are in the air for Chimbulak, however, with the intro-duction of a new high-speed (13 minute) gondola (expected to open for the 2007–08 season) that will run from Medeo (further down the valley) to Chimbulak, and will minimize traffic in the resort. In addition, two new quad chairs will replace the two current double chairs and the one single chair, which could well bring a hike in lift prices. A new hotel is currently under construction in Chimbulak which is expected to open in the autumn of 2010. The current on-site hotel will remain open until the end of the 2007–08 season, with rooms starting at 9,000 tenge.

Smaller resorts outside Almaty include Almatau and Tabagan to the east, although there is no public transport to these resorts. A lavish new resort, Ak Bulak, has recently been built near Talgar, but the facilities are poor at present.

SPAS & BATHS

The Ankara Spa, InterContinental Almaty, 181 Zheltoksan St (Timiryazev), Bostandyk
Tel: 250 5000 ext. 2405 or 2406
Open: daily, 6am–midnight

The well-established Ankara Spa at the InterContinental offers a number of relaxing and rejuvenating massages and treatments in addition to facilities that include a Turkish *hammam*, swimming pool, sauna, a fitness centre, aerobics, tennis courts and more.

Arasan Public Banya, 78 Tulebaev St (Aiteke Bi), Medeu
Tel: 269 2598 or 262 3215
Open: 8am–10pm. Closed Mondays.

An Almaty institution, the Arasan Public Banya (baths) are the perfect way to relax on a cold winter's day when temperatures can reach as low as −15 degrees. Choose between Russian/Finnish or Turkish baths. The former offers a traditional dry Finnish sauna while the former is a large steam room with dark wood-panelled walls, where you can beat yourself with *vyenikki* (birch leaf branches) or simply relax in the heat before descending to the large round pool beneath one of the building's elegant domes. For a different effect, try the Turkish *banya*, in a separate section, where you lie on marble platforms heated to various temperatures. In both sections it is possible to get a massage, though be warned that these are fairly aggressive. Private *banyas* for up to four people are also available where you can even bring in beer and food and make a party of it. The entrance to these private rooms is on Kunaev Street. Tickets for all sections of the *banya* are bought in the basement of the building on Aiteke Bi Street. Sessions start at 8am and continue through the day at two-hourly intervals until 8pm; they cost between 500 and 1,000 tenge depending on the time of day you visit. It is advisable to take flip-flops, a towel, shampoo and a headscarf for women, although you can hire these at the *banya* for a small sum.

Bali Spa Center, Grand Tien Shan Hotel, 115 Bogenbai Batyr (Kunaev), Central Almaty
Tel: 244 9600

The Bali Spa Center, on the lower ground floor of the Grand Tien Shan Hotel in Central Almaty, is an absolute treat. Decorated in neutral tones with a smiling Buddha looking on, the natural wood, bamboo and flowing fountains bring together the elements in a way that soothes and relaxes even before you've begun any of the treatments the spa has on offer. Choose from the gym, Jacuzzi, plunge pool, steam room, sauna and fabulously tiled circular Turkish *hammam*, plus seven separate treatment rooms offering facials, manicures and pedicures, and mud wraps. Once you're really relaxed – why not avail yourself to what the Bali Spa Centre is best renowned for – a Balinese massage extraordinaire, which will leave you with a sense of complete wellbeing.

Club Olympus Spa and Fitness Centre, Hyatt Regency Almaty, 29/6 Satpaev Avenue, Bostandyk
Tel: 250 1234
Open: daily, 6am–11pm

The Club Olympus Spa at the Hyatt Regency Hotel is renowned for being one of the best fitness clubs and spas in town. The club offers an indoor swimming pool, sauna and *hammam* and fitness facilities, as well as (in the summer) tennis courts.

Luxor Wellness Club, 341 Dostyk Avenue, Medeu
Tel: 267 7595 or 267 7597 www.luxor.kz
Open: daily, 7am–midnight

The inspiration of the President's youngest daughter, Aliya Nazarbayeva, Luxor Wellness Club was built after she visited Egypt and fell in love with its temples. Located on Dostyk as the road heads up towards the mountains, the Luxor Wellness Club, with its hieroglyphic murals and statues of sphinxes and gods inside, has a certain *je ne sais quoi* about it, possibly because it's a small, incongruous chunk of Egypt in the heart of Kazakhstan (complete with its own Rameses Restaurant). However, Luxor, as its name also suggests, delivers luxury (and wellness) – at a price. If you need somewhere to relax from Almaty's hectic pace, Luxor's spa and beauty centre, which offers a variety of massages and other relaxation treatments, could be just the ticket. Please note that access to their fitness centre, pool and sauna is for members only – which will set you back roughly 76,000 tenge a month.

Astana

Kazakhstan's capital, Astana, is situated over 1,000km to the northwest of Almaty in the middle of the steppe. Founded as a Russian military outpost in 1824, in 1868 the outpost was expanded, becoming an administrative centre named Akmolinsk. In the 1950s the city became Tselinograd (City of the Virgin Lands), centre of Kruschev's ultimately doomed campaign to grow wheat on the Kazakh steppe. At this time it developed into a small urban centre, home to many of the thousands of Russians, Ukrainians and Belorussians who came to work the 'Virgin Lands'. After Kazakhstan gained its independence in 1991, the city was renamed Akmola, changing once again to Astana (meaning 'capital' in Kazakh) in 1997 during the transfer of the capital from Almaty.

The reasons for the move are much debated, with theories ranging from a desire to establish a more Kazakh presence in the slav-dominated north of the country, to wanting to move away from earthquake-prone Almaty. What is certain, however, is that the new capital has given the government an opportunity to create a monumental capital – a symbol of Kazakhstan's growing importance in the world economy, with its natural resource wealth reflected in the city's many mirrored skyscrapers. If you fly in to Astana, the city rears up out of nowhere, its shiny skyscrapers a stark contrast to the vast emptiness of the surrounding steppe.

Designed, in part, according to a masterplan by renowned Japanese architect Kisho Kurokawa, the old city of Astana sits to the north of the River Ishim (Esil in Kazakh) while new Astana is under construction on the Left Bank, to the south of this river. With Astana's oil-fed construction boom, the population has more than doubled to 600,000 since the capital's move, and is expected to reach one million by 2030 – a significant date in Kazakhstan's long-term development strategy.

The many businessmen and officials who have made the city their home did not universally welcome the move to Astana. With temperatures reaching –40°C during the long winter months compounded by strong steppe winds, many residents still enjoy returning to Almaty at the weekends.

In many ways, however, Astana has achieved its goal of cementing a Kazakh-dominated national identity for this young nation. Walk along the new city's central boulevard and you will find yourself surrounded by local tourists who have come from other parts of the country to wonder at their new place in the world.

With the official move of all the embassies from Almaty to Astana by the end of 2006, the pace of new construction and the availability of new services have accelerated. In fact, it is hard to keep up to date as new restaurants, bars and nightclubs open every week. This growth is a positive development with an increase in available services leading to a much greater choice. Astana is not yet a hedonists' paradise, but watch this space.

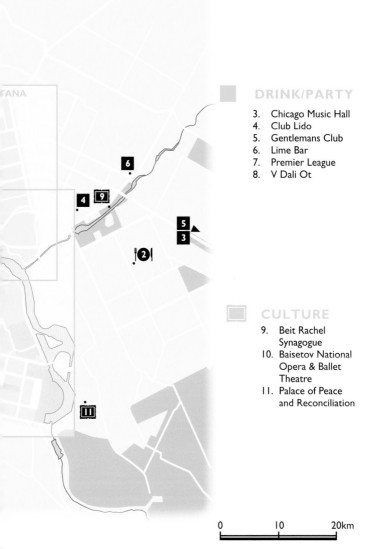

DRINK/PARTY

3. Chicago Music Hall
4. Club Lido
5. Gentlemans Club
6. Lime Bar
7. Premier League
8. V Dali Ot

CULTURE

9. Beit Rachel Synagogue
10. Baisetov National Opera & Ballet Theatre
11. Palace of Peace and Reconciliation

0   10   20km

Right Bank

Situated to the north of the River Ishim, Astana's Right Bank (the old town) is a mix of Tsarist buildings, Soviet blocks and modern skyscrapers. The rate of construction here is as fast-paced as on the Left Bank, although less dominating, thanks to an already developed city centre.

The Right Bank is bordered by the Ishim River to the south, which was widened in the 1960s by the creation of a dam to create a more substantial river frontage. A walk along the embankment is a pleasant experience: in the summer, you can watch residents canoe along the river or take a ride in antiquated paddle boats; in winter the river is the heart of the city once more as men sit fishing on the ice, and inhabitants dig out their cross-country skis and slide along the snow-covered ice. It is even possible to join in by hiring a pair of skis and boots at one of the small kiosks on the riverbank.

At the southwest corner of the Right Bank, where Sary Arka Avenue crosses the river, the newly built Radisson Hotel looks out over the water towards new Astana. One of the city's best hotels, the Radisson couldn't be better located for nocturnal hedonists for the simple reason that Chocolate – Astana's best nightclub – is located in the same building.

From the Radisson, walk along Sary Arka, turn east up Abai Street and you will reach the heart of the Right Bank, passing by the post-independence Ministry of Finance, built in the shape of a dollar, and the Museum of the First President of the

Republic of Kazakhstan, President Nazarbayev's residence until he moved to the Left Bank in 2001. Further up Abai you will come to the Old Square, dominated by the Ministry of Tourism at one end and the Congress Hall at the other. You will also find Tsum here, the central

state shop recently renamed Sine Tempore Shopping Mall. Also situated on the Old Square is the Grand Park Esil Hotel, an attractive 19th century building which is perfectly located for people who prefer to stay in the old town.

Two blocks east of the Old Square, Respublik Prospect runs from the river northwards and is the backbone of the Right Bank, home to the President's Cultural Centre, the small but worthwhile Museum of Modern Art and a number of Astana's restaurants and bars.

Walk around the Right Bank and among the newer buildings you will discover shuttered wooden houses with intricate wooden fretwork hanging from their windows – the most notable of which is the Seifullin Museum at the intersection of Seifullin and Auezov streets.

One important thing to be aware of is that many of the streets in the old town have had their numbering system redesignated. Don't be surprised to find that number 80 is now number 32. We have used the new numbers, which correspond with the numbers you will see attached to the newer signs.

0   5   10km

SNACK

27. Bar Fontan
28. Corso Café
29. Fifty-Fifty
30. La Belle
31. Pizza City

DRINK/PARTY

17. Beerleader
18. Che Guevara
19. Chocolate
20. Cigar Bar
21. Havana
22. Hollywood City
23. North Wind
24. Seoul Plaza
25. Why Not Lounge Bar
26. Yes Club

Left Bank

Astana's Left Bank represents the heart of President Nazarbayev's vision for his new republic. Almost entirely built since the move of the capital to Astana in 1997, the on going construction on the Left Bank is both relentless and monumental.

The Left Bank is dominated by the 100-metre wide Central Boulevard which stretches for over a mile between Kazakhstan's two axes of power – the building of the state oil and gas company, KazMunaiGas, in the west and the Presidential Palace in the east, taking in the Ministries of Defence and Foreign Affairs, the National Library, Parliament and the Courts of Justice on the way.

In 2006, the main axis was further extended with the positioning of Norman Foster's new Palace of Peace and Reconciliation across the river from the Presidential Palace, and the initial stages of construction of another Foster commission – a giant indoor tent, Khan Shatyr – to the west of KazMunaiGas. These two structures, both of which will have been built in record time, look set to be the architectural high-lights of the new city, along with Manfredi Nicoletti's boat-shaped con-cert hall, currently also under construction.

To really appreciate the scale of the building work, walk to the middle of the Central Boulevard and ascend to the top of Baiterek or the 'tree of life' – a large glass sphere perched atop a 100-metre-tall tower representing the Kazakh national myth of a golden egg laid by the leg-endary Kazakh bird Samruk. From this vantage point, you can see the scale of Astana's construction, as cranes and skyscrapers rise all around you – a frenetic contrast to the emptiness of the surrounding steppe.

Due to open in the autumn of 2008, Foster's second commission in Astana, Khan Shatyr – a giant indoor city with its own beach made with solar-trapping materials – looks set to become a year-round paradise for sun-worshipping hedonists: even when it is –30°C on the snow-covered steppe outside.

Other buildings of note on the Left Bank are the central mosque, funded by a Qatar-based prince, the circus on Kabanbai Batyr, whose circular form is reminiscent of a UFO, and, just behind

this, the huge neo-Stalinist style residential 'Triumph' tower – an interesting style of construction in an area which was the location for some of Stalin's most notorious gulags in the 1940s and 50s on the steppe outside the city.

With the city on the Left Bank springing out of the steppe, street names have not necessarily kept up, and you will find that many of the streets here are numbered rather than named.

Amid all the construction, new green spaces are also being developed, the most obvious being the city's central park, which lies to the south of the River Ishim and is home to an aqua park, an amusement park for children, a roller coaster and even Astana's very own 'Eye'.

CULTURE

14. Atameken Ethno-Memorial Complex
15. Astana Baiterek Monument
16. Nur Astana Mosque

SHOP

17. Sary Arka Shopping Centre
18. MegaCentre

PLAY

19. Rixos Royal Spa
20. VIP Sauna Emir

0   5   10km

sleep...

Perhaps even more so than in Almaty, hotels in Astana are geared towards the businessman – a characteristic reinforced by the fact that they tend to fill up when President Nazarbayev is in town. Currently the three smartest hotels available are the Intercontinental on the Right Bank, which was recently eclipsed by the opening of the newer, fresher Radisson (below) on the banks of the River Ishim. Located on the Left Bank, the Turkish-run Rixos is probably Astana's most luxurious hotel, although perhaps not the best destination for gourmet food.

Although names such as 'The Comfort Hotel' and 'The Business Hotel' may sound off-putting, some of Astana's smaller hotels have more charm than their larger counterparts. Two of our favourites are The Comfort Hotel on the Left Bank and Akky on the Right Bank, just a short walk from the river. Be prepared for reproduction furniture.

A new development on Sary Arka Prospect on the Left Bank will see four or five new neighbouring hotels connected to a series of themed restaurants, which should be completed by the beginning of 2008.

Service is generally okay and tends to be more personal, although not necessarily faultless, in the smaller hotels and more efficient in the larger ones. The concept that the customer is always right is still a new one in this fast-developing country.

Akky Hotel, 22 Ryskulov St (Pobeda), Sary Arka
Tel: 752 700
Rates: 16,000–37,000 tenge

Tucked away behind Kenesary Street and only a short walk from the Right Bank of the River Ishim is the Akky Hotel. The Akky's (Kazakh for white swan) 28 comfortable but business-like rooms include six suites each enhanced with large sitting areas, dining tables and reproduction-style furniture, and the hotel's spacious lobby, friendly staff and sun-filled restaurant offer good-value accommodation and personal service. Located off the main

drag, the Akky is a quiet haven to relax in. After a full day of meetings head down to the swimming pool or sauna for a bit of rejuvenation, or just walk outside and you're only five minutes from the river, where a late afternoon or early morning stroll provides a different perspective on a city that seems always on the go.

Style 7, Atmosphere 7, Location 7

Arman Kala Hotel, 30 Naberezhnaya St (Respublik), Sary Arka
Tel: 221 517 or 222 199
Rates: 15,000–25,000 tenge

You'll find the Arman Kala Hotel just off Respublik Avenue on Naberezhnaya, a quiet little street that gives the hotel an air of peacefulness and provides an escape from the adjacent city centre. The Arman Kala

(Kazakh for dream city) opened in 2004 and offers six rooms on the ground level of a larger building. The hotel brochure describes the rooms as having 'classical Roman style interiors', but they're probably better described as spacious and fairly basic although there's a surprisingly comfortable feel to the hotel. Don't expect any typical hotel services (there's no internet), but they do include breakfast in the room price and can arrange airport transfers. If you're just looking for a standard, well-kept room in a central location, then the Arman Kala is for you. It's located just across from the Museum of Contemporary Art and only a short walk from Tsum and some of the Right Bank's more popular restaurants.

Style 7, Atmosphere 7, Location 8

Astana Park Hotel, Sary Arka Bridge, Central Park
Tel: 556 333   www.astana-park.kz
Rates: 15,360–64,000 tenge

The most unique aspect of the Astana Park Hotel is its location; you'll find it just next to the Central Park on the Left Bank of the River Ishim (directly across the river from the Radisson SAS). The Astana Park Hotel offers a quick escape from the city's turbulent atmosphere with a short walk along the river taking you past Astana's very own beach to the tree-filled Central Park. Offering a billiards club, Elite Club (see Drink/Party) and VIP Sauna Emir (see Play), the Astana Park Hotel's 30 comfortable (yet fairly standard) rooms will give you a different experience on your visit to Astana. Be aware, though, that Elite Club is a popular spot on the weekends and its progressive R&B might not seem appealing if you're trying to catch up on sleep.

Style 6, Atmosphere 7, Location 7

Business Hotel, 18/9 Imanov St (Respublik), Sary Arka
Tel: 223 355 or 222 280 www.business-hotel.kz
Rates: 15,000–29,300 tenge

If you had any doubt as to the most common type of traveller in Astana these days, this hotel's name provides quite a firm clue. The Business Hotel, a small, seven-room hotel with functional accommodation, is conveniently located on the Right Bank, and provides a comfortable alternative to Astana's larger, more corporate hotels. Offering a variety of single, twin and 'lux' rooms, it's suitable for individual travellers or small business groups, who might find it more convenient to rent the entire hotel. With internet access in each room, parking facilities for drivers, an airport transfer service,

and a very friendly and accommodating staff, the Business Hotel offers personal touches in a city that is very business-minded. Step outside and you'll find yourself virtually next door to Corso Café and Pizza City (see Snack) and less than a block from Tiflis' (see Eat) wholesome Georgian cuisine.

Style 7, Atmosphere 7, Location 7

Comfort Hotel, 60 Kosmonavtov Street, Chubary Microdistrict

Tel: 221 022 www.comforthotel.kz
Rates: 22,000–70,700 tenge

'Feels like home' says the marketing material at the front desk, and we've got to agree they have a point. The Comfort Hotel (situated on the Left Bank next to the British and German embassies) is a diminutive two-storey hotel with an incredibly friendly feel; a business centre and internet access make it a quiet option if you're in town for work. As the name suggests the

hotel's 50 rooms are relatively small but comfortable. The bar in the lobby downstairs has snug armchairs, which are good for sinking into after a long day sightseeing or putting deals together, and although you are situated on the Left Bank, you are only a 15 minute walk from some of

Astana's best restaurants – East-West and La Riviere on one side and Satti and Izymi on the other – so you won't go hungry.

Style 7, Atmosphere 7, Location 8

Grand Park Esil, 8 Beibitshilik Street, Sary Arka

Tel: 591 901 www.grandparkesil.kz

Rates: 21,660–91,200 tenge

The Grand Park Esil (previously known as the Hotel Ishim) is situated right in the heart of the Right Bank in the Central Square, which formerly served as the centre of government and is still home to the Ministry of Tourism.

The hotel is uniquely housed in one of Astana's attractive 19th century buildings, and its wide corridors and updated classical decoration make it a charming place to stay; we recommend it for the aesthetes among you. Ideally located for eating out in the old town. On the opposite side of the Central Square, in the corner of the former TSUM and now the Sine Tempore shopping mall, is Venezia (Astana's best Italian restaurant) and just a short walk along Kenesary you will find Line Brew and Vaquero (see Eat).

Style 7, Atmosphere 8, Location 8

Hotel Mukammal, 53/1 Pobeda Street, Sary Arka

Tel: 382 939 www.mukammal.kz

Rates: 10,000–24,000 tenge

Hotel Mukammal is a six-storey, 39-bed hotel located a short walk away from the centre of Astana's Right Bank. It merits inclusion in the guide because of a happy combination of good value for money with the personal touch many of Astana's other hotels seem to lack. Named in honour of the owner's grandmother, who lived through the October Revolution, the Great

Patriotic War, and her husband's posting to Mongolia and China as an attaché, Hotel Mukammal has a homely feeling and good-sized bedrooms. Even the standard singles have a bath, a joy in wintertime when Astana can reach temperatures below –40°C. The owner is welcoming and kind and this filters through to the staff, who are eager to please. The hotel is happy to organise transfers from the airport or the train station.

Style 6, Atmosphere 7, Location 7

Okan InterContinental Astana, 113 Abai Avenue (Respublik), Almaty
Tel: 391 000   www.ichotelsgroup.com
Rates: 36,500–335,500 tenge

The Okan InterContinental Astana is centrally located within walking distance of the Right Bank's restaurants and bars. The first five-star hotel to open in the new capital, the InterContinental has seen better days and now looks slightly tired, however, the comfortably furnished rooms will supposedly undergo renovation sometime soon to keep up with Astana's ever-demanding market. In contrast, the newly renovated Aquarius Health Club is a welcome relief for those looking to end the day with a massage or relaxing in the Turkish *hammam*. The InterContinental's lobby is a popular spot for business meetings among the multitudes of Turkish travellers in Astana, and the hotel houses two tasty restaurants – Puccini's, which serves classic Italian cuisine, and The Eurasia Grill, which specializes in Arabic, Turkish and Kazakh dishes. Connected to the InterContinental is the cosmically themed

Arena Discotheque. Popular among a younger crowd, Arena is open every night (except Monday) from 10pm to 4am.

Style 6, Atmosphere 7, Location 8

Radisson SAS Hotel 4 Sary Arka Avenue, Sary Arka

Tel: 990 000   www.astana.radissonsas.com
Rates: 35,000–427,000 tenge

Located on the Right Bank of the River Ishim, Astana's newest hotel offers five-star luxury and service. Opened in late 2006, the Radisson is part of the large Arman Complex, which includes a business centre, shopping area,

restaurants and the largest World Class Fitness Centre in the CIS (with fitness and spa facilities open to guests). Most of the Radisson's rooms offer stunning views of the river and Astana's constantly changing skyline, while its riverside location allows for lovely walks during Astana's warmer months. Pleasingly, Radisson is the first hotel in Astana to offer *Steppe Magazine* (Central Asia's premier English-language cultural magazine, published by Hg2 Almaty & Astana's authors) in all its rooms. If you're in the market for pure luxury, the Radisson's 18th floor Presidential Suite (by far the most deca-dent suite in Astana) has near 360-degree views of the city and separate sleeping quarters for a security entourage. The Radisson also houses two of Astana's top night spots for when the party mood hits – don't miss the Cigar Bar or Chocolate nightclub (see Drink/Party).

Style 9, Atmosphere 8, Location 9

Rixos President Hotel, 7, 1st Street, Almaty
Tel: 245 050   www.rixosastana.com
Rates: 42,5000–97,500 tenge

Named after President Nazarbayev the Rixos President Astana was the first hotel to be built on the city's Left Bank. Anybody who is anyone in business or government stays here. The huge palm tree and bamboo-filled lobby is the spot to meet, greet and network, and is often filled with trailing spouses too. The hotel's 168 rooms are stylishly decorated in a minimalist fashion, and all have Jacuzzis in the bathrooms and 24-hour free internet access. In addition, every guest is entitled to use the Rixos Spa in the basement, whose dark, chilled-out atmosphere offers a wonderfully refreshing change from the heat (or cold) and construction dust of Astana. While the level of

service is sometimes not up to par, the Rixos' location can't be beaten for business and government meetings in the new heart of Astana.

Style 8, Atmosphere 9, Location 9

eat...

Like the construction activity, the restaurant scene in Astana develops daily. Since 2005 the choice of restaurants available has expanded rapidly and will continue to do so with the opening of a host of new restaurants in the coming months. There are even rumours that Arkady Novikov, Moscow's Conran, will shortly be opening his first restaurant in the city.

The most noticeable feature about eating out in Astana is the high proportion of themed restaurants. Kazakhstan's location at the heart of Eurasia, linking East and West, is reflected in the types of restaurant and the food available – a large number of restaurants offer both a European and an Asian menu, and interiors, waiters and waitresses who will be dressed to match. Many of these restaurants are chains that you will recognize from Almaty, with identikit interiors. These kitrestaurants will soon be augmented by the opening of six new venues on Sary Arka Street on the Left Bank offering Georgian, Russian, Swedish, Korean, Uzbek and Ukrainian food – all the old favourites of world cuisine then. Of the established restaurants, our favourites are La Riviere (below), a large, yellow building located, as its name suggests, by the river on the Left Bank at the entrance to the Central Park, offering very good French cuisine. Across the park on Sary Arka Prospect, another favourite is the Japanese restaurant Mori, and on the Right Bank, Tiflis offers tasty Georgian fare and has a lively atmosphere in the evenings.

Astana Nur, 3/2 Respublik Avenue, Sary Arka
Tel: 223 922 or 223 366
Open: daily, 11am–last guest   6,000 tenge
Caucasian/European

Although the address says that Astana Nur (which translates as Astana Central – don't confuse it with the Central Mosque – Nur Astana) is located on Respublik Avenue, it is actually located just behind Respublik on the footpath running along the bank of the River Ishim. In fact, Astana Nur is the only restaurant in Astana both overlooking the river and capitalising on this position. In the summertime, sit on the covered terrace and watch people

splashing about in canoes and paddleboats below. The view is especially good at sunset and afterwards as the lights of new Astana come on over the water. Astana Nur serves Caucasian and European food and is renowned for offering more than 20 types of *plov* (traditional pilaf) and nearly 50 types of *shashlik* (kebabs). While it attracts a more elite crowd in winter, in the summer the terrace is packed out with an eclectic mix of people who come to enjoy the river at the heart of their city.

Food 8, Service 7, Atmosphere 9

Derby Bar & Grill, 8 Irchenko St, Riverside
Tel: 325 222
Open: daily, noon–2am   5,000 tenge
European/Japanese

With English hunting scenes lining the walls, dark wood-panelled partitions enclosing the tables, and armchairs upholstered in leather, the Derby Bar & Grill aims for a classic English style. Yet despite the English theme, the menu is actually European and Japanese with ingredients flown in from all over the world. The director, Elena Mendina, is a trained sommelier and can provide

excellent pairing advice from Derby's international wine list. As with many of Astana's restaurants, live music starts at 8pm on most nights: saxophone from Tuesdays to Thursdays and jazz on Fridays and Saturdays. If you'd rather eat in peace, it's best to choose a Monday or Sunday – although the music is great if you're in a party mood. Derby Bar & Grill's sophisticated interior and enviable position in the same building as the Radisson means that it attracts a good portion of the local elite and embassy crowd, and it has a river view to boot.

Food 7, Service 7, Atmosphere 7

East-West, 2/2 Kabanbai Batyr Avenue, Almaty
Tel: 243 054
Open: daily, noon–midnight   3,500 tenge
Chinese/Indian/Italian/Kazakh

Designed to bring East and West together in the heart of Eurasia, there's no mistaking the concept behind this restaurant. Partitioned into different sections, you can choose to dine in one of three areas: Kazakh, Indian or Italian and once seated you can then choose from a variety of cuisines: Kazakh, Russian, Chinese, Indian or Italian – each with its very own colour-coded menu (quite possibly Astana's longest). Despite the baffling number of choices on offer, East-West, which stands on the banks of the River Ishim by the bridge connecting Respublik Avenue with Kabanbai Baytr, is actually one of Astana's best restaurants with simple, delicious food cooked up by Indian

executive chef, Sunil Gopal. According to Gopal, it's the Kazakh potatoes that make the gnocchi so mouth-wateringly good, and when you find your-self eating this Italian dish while sitting underneath the crown of a yurt in the restaurant's Kazakh corner, it isn't hard to believe. Surreal but worth a visit.

Food 8, Service 8, Atmosphere 7

Egorkino, 93 Auezov Street, Sary Arka
Tel: 323 878   www.egorkino.kz
Open: daily, 8am–1am   5,500 tenge
Russian

One of Astana's most popular restaurants, Egorkino is, at nine years old, almost as old as the capital itself. There is no mistaking the fact that Egorkino is a traditional Russian restaurant; its nooks and crannies are filled with a riot of Russian trinkets – be they small reed shoes, traditional Russian printed curtains, antique chests, or red- black- and gold- painted enamel wooden mugs. The food is tasty and filling (try 'Granny's Snack' – potato and onion cooked with *sala* or pork lard) but this is not the place to come if you're trying to slim. The Russian waiters and waitresses wear tradi-tional dress and the service is attentive. In the background, you will be treated to some old favourite Russian folk songs such as 'Kalinka Kalinka' interspersed with Russian classics from the 1970s and 80s. Drink a few

shots of vodka, and you'll soon find yourself singing along.

Food 7, Service 7, Atmosphere 8

Farhi, 3 Bokeikhan St (Kenesary), Sary Arka
Tel: 321 899 or 320 406
Open: daily, noon–last guest   5,000 tenge
Kazakh

Opened in 1999, Farhi was the first national Kazakh restaurant in Astana – a fact that was significant enough to ensure that the President himself cut the ribbon. Circular in shape and designed to look like the interior of a Kazakh yurt, albeit one with a disco ball hanging from the ceiling, Farhi serves some of the best traditional food in town, including *solyanka* (a traditional broth-based soup) with horsemeat, which is surprisingly tasty. True to local form, however, the restaurant does not stop at traditional food, also offering

Japanese cuisine including sushi and even, to round off your meal, Yamazaki single malt whisky. In the summer, the adjoining vine-covered terrace becomes the outside restaurant Ali Baba, which also serves traditional Central Asian food, with perhaps more of an emphasis on Uzbek cuisine. As Astana's first traditional restaurant, and given the Kazakh's predilection for their own food, Farhi is always full, guaranteeing an atmospheric experience.

Food 7, Service, 7, Atmosphere 7

Izymi, 32 Kabanbai Batyr Avenue, Kruglaya Ploshad
Tel: 242 723
Open: daily, noon–last guest   8,000 tenge
Japanese

A sister restaurant to neighbouring Satti, Izymi has a Japanese menu and waitresses sporting kimonos and obi sashes with chopsticks in their hair. Because of its location at the heart of the Left Bank, the restaurant is very

popular on weekdays and slightly less busy at weekends. Izymi attracts a chic local crowd in the evenings that come to enjoy some of Astana's best sushi and chat in the quiet, sophisticated surroundings. The minimalist Japanese-style interior offers just eight tables to guests, so get there early if you want to ensure yourself a place. Plans for expansion include a softer, chill-out room next door.

Food 8, Service 7, Atmosphere 8

Korolevskaya Ohota, Near the Eurasia 2 Trade Centre, Microdistrict 4

Tel: 341 817

Open: daily, noon–midnight   12,000 tenge

Eclectic

Despite its odd location at the back of the giant Eurasia shopping centre in microdistrict number four, Korolevskaya Ohota (which translates as the Royal Hunt) is one of Astana's smartest restaurants and the haunt of the super-elite. Serving up trophies of the hunt like venison, quail, duck and wild

boar, this is the place to go if you want to indulge in high-class company. The décor, which is reminiscent of a medieval baron's castle, is complemented by a wide variety of taxidermied animals, some of which, disconcertingly, also appear on the menu. Thankfully, though, the grizzly that greets you with out-stretched claws at the door doesn't make it to your plate.

Food 6, Service 7, Atmosphere 8

La Riviere, 2 Kabanbai Batyr Avenue, Central Park

Tel: 242 260

Open: daily, noon–midnight   10,000 tenge

European

La Riviere stands out among Astana's restaurants – partly because of its position on the banks of the Ishim River in an elegant, classically designed building but more compellingly because of the sophistication that this 'small island of France' exudes. Opened in 2001, La Riviere offers mouthwatering

European cuisine, complemented by an extensive and very impressive wine list. Add to that the stylish blue, white and gold interior laden with chandeliers and crowned by a small glass mosaic dome, and you can see why it's not hard to enjoy yourself in such refined surroundings. The sophistication pays dividends: many government delegations frequent La Riviere. (This means, though, the restaurant has had to branch out into traditional food as well; it seems that a Kazakh is not long parted from his *besparmak*.) La Riviere must be complimented on its attention to detail (from the silver tea trolley serving fresh tea and dried apricots to the Coco Chanel perfume in the loo), and we're happy to report that they also brew the best café latte in town.

Food 9, Service 9, Atmosphere 9

Line Brew, 20 Kenesary St, Sary Arka
Tel: 236 373 or 237 444 www.line-brew.kz
Open: daily, noon–last guest   6,000 tenge
Grill/Steakhouse

Like its counterpart in Almaty, Line Brew's interior is a gothic castle with coats of armour welcoming you at the door – a fitting way to set the scene before toasting the night away to some of the 24 Belgian beers they have on tap. From the outside, however, Astana's Line Brew is completely different. Built on the site of one of the city's former fire stations, the restaurant has incorporated the old red brick tower, which now houses (at the top) a circular VIP room complete with karaoke facilities – perhaps an opportunity to sing like Rapunzel for your prince? As one of Kazakhstan's established

brands, Line Brew is very popular with both locals and foreigners and even, they say, with the President. With its roaring central fire powered by *saksaul*, a desert tree which burns slowly and is the ultimate barbecuing fuel, take your pick of steaks or *shashlyk* and know that you will be well served…and well fed.

Food 8, Service 8, Atmosphere 8

Mori, 3 Sary Arka Avenue, Karaoktel Microsdistrict
Tel: 241 024
Open: daily, noon–midnight   14,000 tenge
Japanese

The highly attractive Mori is exclusively Japanese – a point well worth noting in a city where just about every menu promises every type of cuisine.

(It's nice knowing your sushi chef isn't also preparing fresh gnocchi.) Offering sushi and the only *teppanyaki* kitchen in Astana, Mori uses Japanese minimalism to demonstrate that less is definitely more. Cushioned arm-chairs, bamboo Venetian blinds and dark oriental chests make the restaurant pleasant and unique in a city full of kit restaurants. Located in the Left Bank's Caspi Sports Complex on Sary Arka Avenue, it's well placed if you're staying at the Radisson or some of the Right Bank's smaller hotels. Mori's stylish interior and delectable Japanese food isn't lost on the locals, either. They flock here in droves to enjoy such delicacies as the Kobe beef, lobster, prawns and scallops that are cooked on the *teppanyaki* table in front of them. Busy every night, it's worth booking if you want to ensure a table. Alternatively come for lunch (noon–2pm) when it's slightly less busy and order a bento lunch special for only 3,800 tenge.

Food 8, Service 8, Atmosphere 8

Pivovaroff, 24 Beibitshilik Street, Sary Arka
Tel: 328 866 or 321 981
Open: daily, noon–2am   3,500 tenge
German

This German-style beer house brews its own beer and is one of the most popular beer restaurants (yes – there are quite a few) in Astana, attracting a lively crowd throughout the day and into the evening. Owned by a German

who splits his time between Kazakhstan and Germany, Pivovaroff brews two alcoholic and one non-alcoholic types of beer in the giant copper vats

175

situated in the restaurant's back room. The basement location and exposed brick walls are reminiscent of a Munich beer cellar, an illusion strengthened after ordering Pivovaroff's tasty German sausages. The restaurant's popularity is cemented by the friendly Malian manager, Idris, who arrived in Astana to study and hasn't left yet.

Food 7, Service 8, Atmosphere 7

Satti, 32 Kabanbai Batyr Avenue, Kruglaya Ploshad
Tel: 242 848
Open: daily, noon–last guest   6,000 tenge
European

Satti is one of several restaurants located in the improbably named Round Square situated at the KazMunaiGas end of the Central Boulevard on the Left Bank. Mainly due to its location, Satti attracts top government ministers

and the business elite, while maintaining a relaxed and intimate atmosphere. The building is circular in design so the candlelit tables all look onto a central stage, which is the focal point for a daily music and dance show at 8pm. The food, which is European with a smattering of Kazakh, is tasty, and the restaurant's pastel-toned, contemporary Islamic design works well. In the summer, the restaurant expands in the form of a tented village on the roof; although unsophisticated, it's a good place to come for *shashlik* and a view of the Central Boulevard – especially at night when it's set alight.

Food 6, Service 7, Atmosphere 6

Tiflis, 14 Imanov St (Respublik), Almaty
Tel: 221 226
Open: daily, noon–2am   4,000 tenge
Georgian

Many restaurants in Astana have an admirable way of seeming more like a small village than a restaurant, and Tiflis is no exception. Taking the medieval name of the capital of the Caucasian republic, this Georgian restaurant is buzzing with energy, much like Tiflis (or Tbilisi) itself. Visit in the evening and the atmosphere (on the first floor at least) will be boosted by Tamara, an

ethnic Georgian living in Kazakhstan, who sings Georgian folk songs with a bit of Russian, Armenian and Kazakh thrown in. If you'd rather have a more discreet meal, climb the stairs with carved wooden banisters and dine in the slightly quieter upstairs room. The food, in true Georgian style, is delicious with a varied menu, although be warned that not everything you want is always readily available. The *khachapuri*, Georgian bread filled with *suluguni* cheese, comes in a number of guises and pomegranate seeds are liberally distributed throughout the appetizers. In the summer, there is a more informal café outside, and if you want to do things the traditional Georgian way, order your very own *Tamada*, or Georgian host, to complete your dining experience.

Food 8, Service 8, Atmosphere 8

Tre Kronor, 17 Sary Arka Avenue, Sary Arka
Tel: 402 025
Open: daily, noon–last guest   4,500 tenge
Swedish

Named after the national emblem of Sweden, Tre Kronor (or Three Crowns) is a Swedish-style beer house on Astana's Left Bank that was opened in summer 2007. One of six new restaurants that will ultimately open on this stretch of road, Tre Kronor embraces a wider European remit than its name suggests with its German bratwurst sausages (a house speciality) on the menu and Dutch Breughel murals on the walls. The waiters, however, stick to the Swedish theme, wearing traditional Swedish country dress. Tre Kronor does what a beer house should, providing a wide range of ales on tap, as well as using it to flavour its menu. Adjacent to the restaurant and upstairs is a nightclub that was opened in September 2007. With its Latvian DJ and three circular levels connected with a spiral staircase, guests can relax in plush sofas set against a golden interior watching others dance the night away on the lower-level dance-floor.

Food 6, Service 7, Atmosphere 7

Vaquero, 5 Beibitshilik St (Kenesary), Sary Arka
Tel: 390 121
Open: daily, noon–2am (5am Fri/Sat)   5,000 tenge
Eclectic

Vaquero, which brings a little bit of the Wild West to Astana (not that Kazakhstan's new capital is lacking a frontier mentality), is a popular place to hang out among the Cowboys and Indians, wolf-skins and Aztec-inspired columns. Offering Italian, Mexican, Argentinean and European food, there is definitely something for everybody, although the *fajitas*, *tortillas*, *tacos* and *burritos* are the house speciailties. Pronounced 'Vac-you-aero' in Russian, this

restaurant is popular with a young, hip set who crowd onto the denim-covered bar stools at the weekends. In fact, the restaurant's popularity has prompted the owners to consider starting a chain, with new branches opening soon in Almaty, Karaganda and Atyrau.

Food 6, Service 7, Atmosphere 7

Venezia, 1st Floor, Sine Tempore Shopping Mall, 9 Beibitshilik St, Sary Arka
Tel: 753 906
Open: daily, 11.30am–3pm and 6–11pm   4,500 tenge
Italian

Astana's only dedicated Italian restaurant, Venezia is located in the same building as the Sine Tempore shopping mall on the old square, although the entrance is on Kenesary Street. Giant murals of Canaletto's Venice line the

yellow marbled walls, and greenery is abundantly positioned throughout the restaurant. The classical piano music in the evening is the perfect complement to the genuine Italian food, much of which – salami, *prosciutto*, *parmigiano*, beef, fish and rice – has been imported from Italy to ensure its quality. The buffet lunch is highly recommended, partly because of the delicious *antipasti* and cheeses but also because it's only 2,200 tenge. The Italian chef, who has been working in the restaurant since 2001, makes Astana's best risotto with flavours ranging from artichoke to parmesan and truffles. It's no surprise that Venezia is a favourite among the city's diplomatic community.

Food 8, Service 7, Atmosphere 7

Zhibek Zholy, 102 Abai Avenue (Valikhanov), Almaty
Tel: 210 507
Open: daily, noon–2am   6,500 tenge
Eclectic/International

With its name meaning Silk Road (Zhibek Zholy), you won't be surprised to find a mixture of Chinese, Kazakh, Uzbek and international dishes on the menu. To complement its Silk Road cuisine, the restaurant is elaborately designed in different sections; the downstairs is a bright white Uzbek hall with giant Persian miniatures and Islamic arches decorating the walls, while upstairs is Kazakh themed, complete with columns in the shape of *bal bals* (stone figures found on burial mounds on the steppe) and petroglyphs (rock carvings). The VIP room takes on a Chinese style with a portrait of Mao

Zedong emblazoned on a carpet hanging on one side of the room. There's even a Moroccan section (even though there's no Moroccan food) with plush pillows and filigree lanterns hanging from above – again creating the 'something for everything' feeling that pervades many of Astana's dining establishments.

Food 7, Service, 7, Atmosphere 7

drink/party...

One club in Astana stands out above all the rest and that place is Chocolate (below) – a club that wouldn't look out of place in New York, Paris or London. If you go to Astana and you want to go out, look no further – although be warned that if you want to sit down at one of the alluringly comfortable tables you'll be faced with a hefty minimum drinks spend, so it may be better to prop up the bar instead.

In terms of live music venues, Astana has a couple of options including Yes Club, which plays Russian rock music from the 1970s and 80s for a lively crowd of nostalgic locals.

There are a number of established pubs and beer houses in Astana including North Wind, Chelsea, PivoVaroff, Beerhouse and Baden Baden although many of them lack atmosphere and clientele. If atmosphere is what you are after, our favourite bar is Che Guevara, a small bar located just off Imanov Street where you are likely to meet a creative, non-business crowd. If you want to watch that international football match, try Premier League run by a Chelsea-mad owner.

Astana is also known for a number of strip clubs, all of which offer 'crazy menus' in addition to the show. Perhaps the smartest is the Gentleman's Club at Chicago Music Hall on the Karaganda road. For pure entertainment value, Chicago Music Hall is well worth a visit, too – that is if you like musicals. It's not quite Broadway, but the Kazakh and Ukrainian actors and singers belt out a good song.

Beerleader, 80/1 Sary Arka Avenue, Sary Arka
Tel: 239 740 or 239 997
Open: daily, noon–last client

As soon as you enter Beerleader, it's not hard to know what goes on inside. Beerleader is a football fanatic's dream; the bar is decorated with more football paraphernalia than you would ever know existed – the light coverings and bar are illuminated with different team logos, the walls are plastered with old sports newspapers, team flags line the wall, and each table is

topped off with its own miniature team flag. No matter how obscure your own team is, you're bound to find it represented here. Opened in summer 2007 in the old Up and Down night club, Beerleader broadcasts live football matches, and when there aren't any live matches on, they play films of old Soviet matches or documentaries on the history of Soviet football starting at 8pm nightly. So, if you're in the mood for a bit (or a lot) of football, you're bound to find some kindred spirits at Beerleader.

Che Guevara, 28 Imanov St (Respublik), Sary Arka
Tel: 946 231
Open: daily, noon–2am

If you manage to find this small bar in a courtyard just off Imanov Street and east of Respublik Avenue (turn right between Kamilla and Cleanelly into a courtyard with a grey building at the back and go through the door which says A-Zone Studio), you will be pleasantly surprised. Che Guevera is a popular spot with architects, designers, journalists and artsy-types who come together in this democratic environment to discuss higher things. Che Guevara calls itself a pre-party café and is, according to the owner, a meeting place for free spirits. From the walls, large format photographs of the

ultimate free spirit and Communist hero himself stare down at the assembled crowd, while DJs play the occasional set. On Wednesday nights, DJ Junglist records the 'Night Rhythms' radio show from Che Guevara between 9 and 11pm, and in the summer it's good to check in with the staff at Che Guevara's to find out more about the open air parties that take place on a beach outside Astana. These are organised in conjunction with the website www.nightrhythms.kz and are sure to be debauched as hell.

Cigar Bar, Radisson SAS Hotel, 4 Sary Arka Avenue, Sary Arka
Tel: 990 000
Open: daily, 6pm–4am

While Astana might not have many cozy, corner cafés where you can enjoy the Sunday papers over a cappuccino, it does have a lot of places where a strong whisky can accompany the latest business deal – it's just a function of what makes this city tick: business and politics. That's why the Cigar Bar (situated inside the Radisson Hotel) has become one of Astana's most popular places to end the day. With its dark, wooden panels, elegant décor and red leather couches and chairs, the Cigar Bar has a very intimate atmosphere and feels more like a private club. The special cedar, walk-in humidor ensures the freshness of its Cohibas, Partagas and Monte Cristos that helps

guests to unwind and relax. Popular most evenings, you're sure to see some of Astana's most important movers and shakers puffing away.

Lime Bar, 5/2 Mozhaiskov St, Canalside, Almaty
Tel: 274 671
Open: daily, 11am (3pm Sat/Sun)–1am (3am Fri, 4am Sat)

With its flair bartender, à la Tom Cruise in Cocktail, and lime green walls, Lime is the kind of lounge bar you wouldn't expect in the middle of the steppe. Along with Che Guevara and Chocolate, Lime is one of the best

places to hang out in town. Its themed parties on Friday and Saturday nights draw in the crowds, as do the guest DJs from Almaty and Moscow, including Almaty's best DJ – Rustam Ospanoff.

North Wind, Astana Tower, 1 Respublik Avenue, Almaty
Tel: 223 346
Open: daily, 11am–2am

Opened in 2002, North Wind was one of Astana's first pubs and is still a good place to go on weekdays, although we wouldn't recommend it at the weekend (unless you are looking for peace and quiet). Guinness and Efes are served on tap, and a couple of groups play live music everyday between

8pm and 11pm. The jazz is good fun and not too loud (a unique distinction from most of Astana's drinking establishments). Your fellow drinkers are likely to be businessmen or diplomats looking for a comfortable English pub setting in the middle of the steppe.

Premier League, 5 Timiryazev St (across from the Arsenal Cinema), Sary Arka
Tel: 384 416
Open: daily, 4pm–2am

Premier League calls itself a Soccer Pub and there's no doubt about that. This two-storey building is located just across from the Arsenal Cinema and next to the Agricultural University, which makes it a favourite among students as well as other locals and expats alike. The owner is a self-described Chelsea fanatic, and that becomes pretty clear once you walk inside. Over the years he has amassed a huge collection of Chelsea memorabilia and with nowhere else to display it, he opened Premier League as his own personal shrine to his favourite team. But don't despair if you're colours

aren't blue and gold; fans of all types are welcome and you might even find your own team's flag nestled among Chelsea's. Premier League is extremely popular when big games are on television, so make sure to ring and reserve a table in advance if you don't want to be left standing.

Why Not Lounge Bar, 102 Abai Avenue (Valikhanov), Almaty

Tel: 210 507
Open: daily, noon–last customer

Located on the ground level of Zhibek Zholy restaurant (see Eat), as its name suggests, why not try one of Astana's newest lounge bars? Why Not is a mix between a lounge bar and restaurant but has a surprisingly comfortable vibe to it that encourages its clientele to sit back and relax the night

away. Decorated in neutral tones with iridescent brown-tiled columns, dark wooden furniture, bamboo place mats and white leather chairs, Why Not is popular among a mid-twenties and upwards crowd of Astana's trendiest. Once DJ Fara gets going in the evenings, you'll be sipping away to house and lounge music, and on Thursdays, Why Not offers a cocktail and dessert special called 'Tasty Thursdays'. A selection of Zhibek Zholy's menu is available to order as well as an extensive salad menu whose names remind you where you are – why not try a Baiterek, Astana, Nauruz, Zhailou or Almatinski?

CLUBS

Chocolate, Radisson SAS Hotel, 4 Sary Arka Avenue, Sary Arka
Tel: 990 000
Open: 6pm–4am Tues–Thurs and Sun; 10pm–6am Fri–Sat

Chocolate is hands down the hottest place in Astana. Ask anyone who is anyone in the nation's capital where you can party among the city's smartest and they'll all tell you Chocolate is the place. Face control and fashion control are definitely enforced here, so be sure to look your finest if you're expecting to get in. Chocolate opens as a lounge bar during the week (and on Sundays) when they have a live jazz band in the house, but all inhibitions

are lost on Friday and Saturday nights when the club scene gets going and the specially invited DJs from Almaty, Moscow or Europe start spinning their electro, funky and progressive house tunes. Be warned, though, if you plan to sit and enjoy some of Chocolate's comfy looking lounge chairs and sofas, the table price will set you back a minimum of $500. Next door, a new restaurant is in the works, complete with a Buddha-styled interior design, and if it's anything like Chocolate, it's sure to be a hit.

Elite Club, Sary Arka Bridge, Almaty

Tel: 556 333 www.astana-park.kz
Open: 10pm–5am. Closed Mondays.

Elite Club, located just inside the lobby of the Astana Park Hotel, opened in February 2007 and has been a popular night-time haunt ever since. With the

house DJ spinning progressive R&B tunes, Elite Club attracts a 25+ crowd that dances the night away under the club's bright blue ceilings and on its reflective floors. The red walls accented with gold lame curtains and gold topped Victorian sofas all add to the allure that the club's name exudes; it's all about being part of the elite in Astana. On Friday and Saturday nights, there's a cover charge of 1,000 tenge for ladies and 2,000 tenge for guys, but there's free entry during the rest of the week, and twice a month Elite puts on a local stand-up comedy show – definitely worth checking out if you're in town.

Hollywood City, 22 Koshkarbayev St, Almaty

Tel: 214 249
Open: 10am–5am. Closed Mondays

The rumour on the steppe is that Hollywood City is about to change its name and undergo reconstruction. It's such a common occurrence in this city that there is no reason to disbelieve it, but until it's confirmed, assume you are heading for Hollywood City. The first thing you'll notice, or not if you don't read Cyrillic, is that lots of things are forbidden in this club except

for a Hollywood smile. So wear a big grin and climb the stairs to the disco on the top floor for some more hip hop, R&B and electro-house (music variety in Astana is still quite limited). On weekday nights and Sundays, the club concentrates on TV-based entertainment: football on Sundays, wrestling on Tuesdays, and blue movies on Wednesdays. Take your pick.

Seoul Plaza, 16/2 Respublik Avenue, Almaty
Tel: 328 010 or 328 462
Open: 10pm–5am daily

There are not many clubs in Astana that don't have a striptease, and Seoul Plaza is no exception. This club has two dance halls, but the one downstairs is definitely best. If you get tired of dancing to the house DJ's selection of electro-house, pop and R&B, you can pop upstairs to the billiards hall which is open until 5am. If you're making a night of it, and you happen to be Russian Orthodox, you won't have long to wait after closing until the bells start ringing for the next-door cathedral's first service.

LIVE MUSIC

Havana, 18 Beibitshilik St, Sary Arka
Tel: 910 069
Open: noon–2am (3am Fri/Sat). Closed Sundays.

Viva Piva! says a poster of Che Guevara hanging over the dance-floor at Havana's, a Cuban street-themed club with Havana-style streetlights, palm trees and waitresses wearing Spanish flamenco-style dresses. Between 10pm and 1am every day except Monday and Tuesday, Havana has great sets of live music including classics from the 1980s and 90s, rap and R&B. The crowd here tend to be older than at Chocolate, mainly 30 and above, and generally more democratic – plus, the drinks are cheaper, entrance is free (except when there's live music on), and the outdoor terrace with sofas is a good place to relax if it gets too steamy inside.

Yes Club, 33 Respublik Avenue (Abai), Sary Arka
Tel: 330 214
Open: daily, 6pm–5am

The unassuming entrance to this club, which is attached to the Hotel Abai on Respublik Avenue, belies what is going on inside. Enter to the right and you will find a host of 30 year olds (and over) going wild on the dance floor as various local bands play tunes from their teenage years. Mainly Russian rock, but with some international favourites thrown in, Yes Club is a great place to spend an evening. The walls are crammed full of photos of ageing Russian rockers, some of whom have played at Yes Club, and even if you don't know the tunes you'll find that the music and the atmosphere get your toes tapping. With four years of live music behind them, Yes Club is going strong, and as one of the only venues dedicated to live music in Astana, long may it last.

SHOW

Chicago Music Hall, Karaganda Road, Karaganda Trassa
Tel: 232 323
Open: 9pm–2am (show from 9–11pm) Weds–Sun

Imagine seeing a Broadway musical in the middle of the steppe. Now you can, with the summer 2007 opening of the Chicago Music Hall showing performances of *Chicago*, the musical, which can add Kazakhstan to its long repertoire list. Located on the Karaganda Road just outside the city, you simply can't miss the Chicago Music Hall as it's lit up like a Vegas casino. Inside, the Music Hall oozes glitz and glamour; a shiny white interior and sleek leather couches greet you in the lobby before entering the theatre for a night of dining and dancing. *Chicago* is enthusiastically performed by a Russian/Ukrainian/Kazakh theatre group, and the show is interspersed with jazz performances by the Music Hall's house band, Capital. Tables for four range from 60,000 tenge (for those closest to the stage) to 20,000 tenge a few rows back. Each table comes with a bottle of champagne and a fruit assortment; all other food and drinks can be ordered à la carte from the Music Hall's European-style menu. If you haven't had enough once the musical show is over, head upstairs to the Gentleman's Club (see Strip Clubs) for a different kind of show.

STRIP CLUBS

Club Lido, 194/1 Imanov St, Almaty
Tel: 376 223 or 376 224
Open: daily, 10pm–5am

Another disco-spinning house and R&B tunes with a non-stop striptease in the strip club downstairs, the crazy menu here is said to be especially popular with foreigners.

Gentleman's Club, Karaganda Road, Karaganda Trassa
Tel: 23 23 23
Open: 10pm–5am Weds–Sun

Located on the second floor of the Chicago Music Hall (see Show), the
Gentleman's Club is, by far, the swankiest and sleekest strip club Astana has
to offer. Just to get inside will set you back 10,000 tenge, but the strip show
is sure to please. If you still feel the need for something a little extra, place
an order from the 'crazy menu' to complete your night of debauchery.

V Dali Ot..., 33 Moskovskaya Street, Sary Arka
Tel: 39 36 33   www.club.dali.dj
Open: daily, 10pm–5am (6am Fri/Sat)

V Dali Ot... (From Dali To…) is, as the name suggests, a more than surreal
experience. The main hall has tables for 120 people (and VIP rooms with
sofas upstairs) where you can watch the incongruously named 'Happy
Childhood' strip group strut their stuff or dance to the tunes of Astana's
'best' DJs. If the strip group seem a little tame, you can also check out V
Dali Ot...'s strip hall offering a 'crazy menu' with listings including tequila,
S&M and more. It's your call.

snack...

As a city in development, Astana lacks the cozy corner café that makes the difference between a good and a great Sunday morning. The closest thing is Pizza City. It may sound like a hideous neon chain, but is in fact a small stylish café on the Right Bank (although the service and food are not yet fully in line with Western expectations) whose growing popularity will, hopefully, presage more of the same. If you find yourself on the Left Bank, head for Café Marzipan on the Central Boulevard, which is a good place to relax after some serious sightseeing, or try the lobby in the Rixos, which is one of the most popular meeting places in town and also offers free WiFi access.

With the opening of a number of new shopping malls in 2008, new coffee shops will arrive in Astana including Gloria Jean's, the Turkish answer to Starbucks.

There are a number of café-style restaurants in Astana including Kishlak and Samovar (below) at the KazMunaiGas end of the Central Boulevard, both of which offer quick, tasty food and are great for more informal lunches.

Bar Fontan, Sine Tempore Shopping Mall, 1st Floor, Kenesary Street, Sary Arka
Tel: 753 906
Open: daily, 10am–10pm

For a small café in the middle of a shopping mall, Bar Fontan is surprisingly popular whatever time of the day you visit. Serving juice, cocktails, cakes, salads and pizzas, this buzzing little café is run by the nearby Venezia restaurant (see Eat), and is a good place to drop into if you're tired from walking

around the old town on the Right Bank. The menu (apart from the pizzas) is in Russian and the staff do not speak English, but it's not hard to get your intentions made clear in a coffee shop, especially since there's no chance of getting a hazelnut triple shot skinny latte here – just espresso and cappuccino.

Café Marzipan, 1 Magistralnii Street (by the Square of the Singing Fountains), Almaty
Tel: 8 701 551 4897
Open: daily, 10am–2am

Opened in May 2007, Café Marzipan is the first coffee shop to open on the Left Bank. A great place to pop in for a fresh juice if you're sightseeing along the monumental Central Boulevard and situated only a few minutes walk from the President's White House and Baiterek, Café Marzipan offers a lunchtime menu of snacks and sandwiches (as well as a 15% discount). From November 2007, there are plans to offer free WiFi, so if you need to get

connected, this could be the place to catch up on your emails. The comfy orange sofas and spacious interior translates well into a night-time spot when the café is at its busiest, serving cocktails to exhausted civil servants who work nearby.

Corso Café, 18 Imanov St (Respublik), Almaty
Tel: 221 249
Open: daily, 10am–1am

Busiest at lunchtime and after the 9pm watershed, Corso Café is located in the heart of Astana's Right Bank. While this comfy café is still some way off the ultimate 'cosy corner café', it is one of the very few cafés Astana has to offer. In some ways it's more like a small bar than a café, with its smoky atmosphere and the fact that it serves alcohol until well after midnight. An

attractive feature is that it serves a simple menu of breakfast and desserts from 10am. Located next to Tiflis (see Eat), it's a nice place to pop in and finish the evening off with a cappuccino (or nightcap) and something sweet.

Fifty-Fifty, 16 Respublik Avenue, Almaty

Tel: 215 858

Open: daily, noon (2pm Sun)–midnight (2am Sat)

Fifty-Fifty refers to Kazakhstan's geographical location between Europe and Asia, and explains why the food on offer is both Eastern (Japanese) and European, a fact that most restaurants in town don't bother to offer any explanation for. At any rate, Fifty-Fifty is a good place to pop into on

Respublik Avenue, the main street in the old town, if you're having sushi withdrawal in the heart of the steppe. The sushi menu has all the usual rolls and sashimi, and there's even a room for children with pint-sized tables and chairs. To round off your meal why not try the Japanese ice cream or cherry and lemon cakes.

Kishlak, 22/2 Kabanbai Batyr Avenue, Kruglaya Ploshad

Tel: 974 161 or 974 142

Open: daily, noon–2am

A sister venture to the Russian Samovar next door, Kishlak, which means village, is just as the name suggests. Walk in over a stream, past a tree and

enter a small Central Asian courtyard with raised platforms, carved pillars, painted and decorated beams, trellises covered with vines and pictures of the Uzbek town of Khiva painted on the walls. The waiters wear *tipitecas* (Uzbek caps) and the waitresses wear *ikat* printed *kurtas* and pink silk trousers. In view of the décor, we think it's worth sticking to the Eastern food on the menu, although European food is also available. Try the *laghman* – a local noodle dish which can be fried or steamed and is served in attractive earthenware dishes from Uzbekistan. The *lepioshka*, Uzbek bread with onion seeds, is delicious and reminiscent of fresh bread from the bazaar in Samarkand. On weekdays Kishlak attracts an older business crowd, which becomes progressively younger, and more rowdy, at the weekends.

La Belle, 12 Irchenko Street, Sary Arka
Tel: 230 600   www.labelle.kz
Open: noon–midnight (2am Thurs–Sat). Closed Sundays.

With its exposed glazed brick walls, shuttered windows with flower-filled window boxes, and murals of French street scenes, La Belle café aims to convince that you're actually sitting in the heart of Montmartre. If that's not enough francophilia, they play French classical music and serve 50 different types of coffee and over 35 types of *chai*, or should we say *thé*? As the city's very first coffee shop, La Belle is unique (at least for Astana) and does not serve food, unless you count a host of tasty-looking desserts, and concentrates instead on perfecting its variety of speciality coffees to keep you warm once the temperature starts to drop. Only a short walk from the Radisson Hotel, La Belle offers WiFi (free for the first hour) and also has a

spa by the same name next door (just in case that cappuccino gets you thinking about a massage).

Pizza City, 17 Imanov St (Respublik), Almaty
Tel: 200 965
Open: daily, 8am–2am

While the name may not have most clamouring at the door, Pizza City has to be the hippest café in town. Its refreshingly cool interior with red and gold lotus-printed wallpaper, stark white tables and chairs, bright orange mats, and low-slung red leather sofas could come straight from the heart of New York City. Understandably so, Pizza City attracts a trendy crowd who come to drink and eat the eponymous pizzas and pasta late into the night. Time your visit earlier (Pizza City opens at 8am daily), and take advantage of some peace and quiet, as well as tucking into their continental breakfast

with croissants and jam, muesli and yoghurt, and fresh fruit. It may not be the Ritz, but it certainly is ritzy; if you want to see Astana à la mode (or just sip on a cappuccino), we highly recommend it.

Samovar, 22/2 Kabanbai Batyr Avenue, Kruglaya Ploshad
Tel: 974 171
Open: daily, noon–2am

Samovar is a *traktir*, the Russian equivalent of an Italian *trattoria* or a French bistro. It achieves this status partly through homely surroundings divided into a number of small rooms, and partly through a menu of home-cooked favourites. It's a great place for lunch; you can sit back in a wood-panelled room with an old Russian-tiled stove in the corner and choose from a wide selection of *blinis* (pancakes), soups and meat dishes prepared in a hot

skillet. To complement your meal, try some *compote*, a traditional Russian juice made from stewed fruits, or if you fancy a lunchtime vodka shot, they'll even give you a piece of lemon with coffee and sugar on it to bite after-wards – apparently a Russian tradition…If you're not on the Left Bank at lunchtime, you can visit a second, slightly less formal, branch of Samovar on the Right Bank at 24 Kenesary Street (just past the Sine Tempore Shopping Mall).

Notes & Updates

culture...

Astana is a city with a potted history, which if you reach back far enough includes steppe nomads, Russian settlers, Stalinist gulags and the founding of a brand new Republic. The museum within the Presidential Cultural Centre will walk you through much of this and is well worth the visit as a result.

To see the making of a new republic in action, just walking around Astana will suffice, but one of the most interesting excursions is to Norman Foster's Palace of Peace and Reconciliation, a 62-metre glass pyramid completed in autumn 2006. It is possible to take a guided tour of the structure which houses a Museum of Gold and Precious Metals from Kazakhstan and a 1,500-seat opera house in the basement.

Otherwise, an interesting way to take in the culture is in the city's theatres and Opera House where the season of plays, concerts, operas and ballets begins in September and runs all the way through the cold winter to June.

Perhaps the best way to get to grips with Kazakhstan's built heritage and geographical diversity is through a visit to the Atameken Ethno-Memorial Complex where a giant 'model' map of Kazakhstan allows you to take in Kazakhstan's cultural monuments in one go.

In fact, not only can you visit remote parts of Kazakhstan in the heart of Astana, it is also possible in winter (December-March) to visit some of the world's most famous cultural monuments when an ice city emerges between the Duman Entertainment Centre and the river. A truly impressive sight, ice sculptures of the Pyramids at Giza, the Eiffel Tower and even Baiterek (below) itself are on display.

Astana Baiterek Monument, Central Boulevard, Left Bank
Open: daily, 10am–7pm

One of the first construction projects in Astana, Baiterek ('Tree of Life') the imposing 97-metre-tall tower (97 reflecting the year the capital was moved to Astana) in the middle of the Central Boulevard, has become the unequivocal symbol of the young capital. The tower holds a spherical glass and metal observation tower in its centre that symbolizes a Kazakh legend in which the mythical bird Samruk (symbolizing happiness) lays a golden egg in a poplar tree. From this observation tower, you gets a bird's eye view of this newly constructed city, which, when looked at from above, appears to have been dropped in the middle of the steppe. Built at the behest of the President, the golden imprint of the President's hand which stands at the centre of this observation tower may be the closest you'll ever come to shaking hands with him.

Nur Astana Mosque, 2nd Street, Almaty

Designed by a Lebanese architect, built by a Turkish company and a gift from the Emir of Qatar, Astana's Central Mosque is a thoroughly Muslim affair. The mosque's central golden dome and four gold-capped minarets complement the white marble exterior, which was finished and officially opened by the President in 2005. Inside, Kazakh artists have done a great job of painting the pastel-toned interior and prayers are held five times a day. If you can, visit at lunchtime on a Friday, when the mosque bursts at the seams as suited businessmen and government ministers mingle with bearded Muslims in tracksuits. One of 1,700 mosques built in Kazakhstan since Independence, the renaissance of Islam is interesting to behold.

Atameken Ethno-Memorial Complex, Kabanbai Batyr, Molodezhni Microdistrict
Tel: 221 636
Open: daily, 10am (4pm Mon)–10pm (March–October)

The Atameken Ethno-Memorial Complex comprises a monument to those who died in Soviet times as a result of political repression, which stands on a small hill at the river end of Kabanbai Batyr. Behind this is a giant 'model' map of Kazakhstan where the Caspian Sea has been reduced to the size of a small pond. The map highlights Kazakhstan's architectural monuments in miniature as well as dedicating a somewhat disproportionately large area to a plan of Astana. It's a good way of getting round a country five times the size of France in half an hour.

Beit Rachel Synagogue, Imanov St (Gumilyev), Almaty

Opened in 2004, the Beit Rachel synagogue in Astana serves a Jewish community of roughly 150 families, most of which originally settled in the area in the 1950s from Belorussia, Lithuania and the Ukraine during Khruschev's Virgin Lands Campaign. The synagogue was funded by businessman Alexander Mashkevich, head of the Eurasian Group and a pal of the President, and is named in honour of Mashkevich's late mother.

The Cathedral of Saints Konstantin and Elena, 16/3 Respublik Prospect, Almaty
Open: daily, 8am–8pm; services: 8.15am and 4.30pm

Built in 1854, this small cathedral tucked just behind Respublik Street has been functioning as a church again since 1999. It is currently acting as Astana's main cathedral until the Orthodox community finds the funds to complete the Saint Uspenski Cathedral, which is under construction.

Central Park and the Ishim River

Astana's Central Park lies on the Left Bank of the Ishim River and, like the embankment path that lies on the right-hand side of the river running from Respublik Street to Sary Arka, is a very pleasant place to take a walk. Although a little jaded, Central Park has an aqua park, a zoo, roller coasters, a ferris wheel and even donkey rides and a beach. You could almost be forgiven for thinking you were in Blackpool. Perhaps more appealing are the slightly antiquated paddleboats which can be hired between June and September between midday and 9pm.

Museum of Contemporary Art, 3/1 Respublik Avenue, Samal Microdistrict, Sary Arka
Tel: 215 433
Open: 10am–5pm (4pm Sun). Closed Mondays.

Tucked away on Respublik Street about three blocks north of the bridge which crosses the river, the unassuming entrance to the Museum of Modern Art belies the interesting (if small) collection inside.

Museum of the Presidential Cultural Centre, 1 Barayev St, Almaty
Tel: 223 308
Open: 10am–6pm. Closed Mondays.

The better of Astana's two museums named after the President (the other one being more of a paean to the President than a museum), this is worth visiting if you haven't been to the Central State Museum in Almaty. Unfortunately, the life-size statue of the golden man is only a replica of the golden costume found in a *kurgan* (tomb) at Issik, near Almaty, as is the reconstruction on the ground floor of equine armour found at Berel. However, since it's not possible to see the real golden man, it's well worth at least having a look at this dramatic costume, even if it is a copy. The shop on the ground floor has some of the best arts, crafts and carpets available in Astana. Because there is no information available in English, take advantage of the free English tour guide if you have the time.

Palace of Peace and Reconciliation, 7 1st Street, Almaty
Tel: 744 744
Open: daily, 10am–7.30pm

Built to host the Congress of Leaders of World and Traditional Religions, the 62-metre-high Palace of Peace and Reconciliation is one of two buildings in Astana designed by the UK's Norman Foster. Completed in an incredible 21 months, it is well worth taking a guided tour. The Pyramid is organized around a central atrium with elevators that take people up along the inward leaning walls to a transparent apex. Just below the Pyramid's peak, designed with blue and yellow stained glass (representing the colors of the Kazakh flag) and embellished with images of doves – the international symbol of peace – sits a circular chamber modelled on the United Nations Security Council. Leading up a winding staircase to this chamber, which serves as the meeting space for the conference delegates, are walls covered in lush vegetation. In addition to representing the world's religious faiths, the Pyramid also houses a research centre dedicated to the study of the world's religions, a library, a museum for Kazakhstan's ethnic groups, offices and a 1,500-seat opera house – a last minute request by the president. The opera house, in the Pyramid's lower level, has a circular glass ceiling that partially illuminates its chamber with light flooding through from the apex above, creating a sense of connection between the lowest level and the top of the building.

THEATRES AND CONCERT HALLS

Baisetov National Opera and Ballet Theatre, 10 Akzhaik St, Sary Arka
Tel: 392 761 or 392 766
Box office opening hours: daily, 10am–7pm

The season at the Opera and Ballet Theatre opens on 12 October and continues until 7 July. The theatre has a repertoire of over 30 different operas and ballets, including *Aida*, *Tosca*, *Swan Lake*, *Evgenii Onegin*, *Giselle* and provides the perfect antidote to a cold Astana winter.

Russian Drama Theatre, 72 Bigeldinov St, Sary Arka
Tel: 328 823 or 320 570
Box office opening hours: daily, 10am–1pm and 2–6pm

The season at the Russian Drama Theatre runs from October to June and tickets costs between 400 and 1,200 tenge. Although all the plays are in Russian, it's an interesting place to see plays by masters such as Chekov, Lermontov, Gogol, Dostovesky and even Shakespeare.

Notes & Updates

Hg2 Almaty & Astana

shop...

Astana is a city of the future and shopping is no exception. Shopping in the capital is currently restricted to large trade centres in the microdistricts, but things, as they say, are changing. The opening of a number of new shopping malls by early 2008 will bring a welcome addition of international brands to the capital.

Capital Partners, the Almaty-based real estate development company, well-known for its high-end, luxury projects in Almaty and Astana, is taking the lead with the opening of the Sary Arka shopping complex in winter 2007 on Astana's Left Bank. Sary Arka will introduce brands such as Nike, Timberland, Beauty Planet, Esprit, Adidas, and even Apple to the capital's anxious and consumer-ready customers. Not only will Sary Arka be first up market mall to provide shopping relief, but will also house an eight-screen cinema and will introduce Il Patio Pizza and Planeta Sushi to Astana's restaurant scene (two favourites among Almaty regulars). Perhaps, the most anticipated of Sary Arka's new tenants is Hediard, the classic Parisian gourmet food and luxury gift store that is sure to take Astana by storm.

Just beyond Sary Arka (also on the Left Bank) is the Mega Center Astana, whose opening will include a new Ramstore (the well-respected Turkish supermarket chain) that's the place to go when in need of basic essentials.

One of the largest construction projects in Astana is Khan Shatyry, the giant transparent tent that will contain an indoor city. Located at the end of the Central Boulevard on the Left Bank and just behind the KazMunaiGas complex, Khan Shatyry is the second of Norman Foster's colossal projects in Astana, and is set to become the world's largest tent. It will have a 500 ft high dome and will be constructed from a material that absorbs sunlight and creates a summer-like temperature year round.

Covering an area larger than ten football stadiums, Khan Shatyry will be a city with cobbled streets and squares, and will have an urban-scale internal park, shopping and entertainment venues, a golf course, sidewalk cafés, restaurants and an indoor beach resort. With construction expected to be completed in late 2008, the residents of Astana will soon have a year round summer shopping paradise, even when it's −30°C outside on the snow-covered steppe.

If you are looking for something more traditional, the best place is the small shop at the museum of the Presidential Cultural Centre at the river end of Respublika Avenue. Additionally, there is a small shop called Art Deco located in the Okan Shopping Centre (just next to the Okan InterContinental Hotel) that offers some new and antique carpets, a small selection of books on Kazakhstan,

and some other Central Asian handcrafts. A stroll through the Sine Tempore Shopping Centre offers a small selection of Kazakh-themed goods as well as more internationally recognized brands. Perhaps better known, but only if you want to buy traditional kitsch (think fluorescent coloured Baiterek lighters, Golden Man key chains and Kazakh-themed shot glasses), is Talisman on Respublika (not far from the Museum of Contemporary Art).

At the time of print, there are not enough individual shops to include a separate shopping section, but get ready because we know things in Astana move faster than we can keep track of. Keep your eyes open as you pass through the capital, and in the meantime, revel in a wonderful break from consumerism...

play...

There are a number of ways to relax in Astana including golf, tennis, ice-skating and swimming. With temperatures routinely reaching −30°C in the winter, visiting the sauna and Russian *banya* at the Sary Arka Public Baths and the *hammam* at the Spa at the Rixos are foolproof ways of warming up.

If you prefer to be outside in the cold weather, try a spot of cross-country skiing along the River Ishim. Where else can you say you've skied a river? Or perhaps you would prefer to amuse yourself in the Ice City that appears between December and March next to the Duman Entertainment Centre, with replicas of some of the world's most famous buildings.

Located in the centre of northern Kazakhstan, Astana is also the perfect jumping-off point for exploring more of this vast country. From Astana you can visit any of a large number of towns including Petropavlosk, Karaganda, Semey, Pavlodar and even Oskemen (formerly Ust-Kamenogorsk) – the gateway to the Altai.

Alternatively, head out into the steppe. If you go to Lake Tengiz, part of the Korgalzhyn National Park, or to the Kokshetau National Park, you can experience real life by staying with local families – something that will add immeasurably to your understanding of Kazakhstan and provide a welcome contrast to the fast pace of development in Astana. These areas are also a paradise for nature lovers and may even convert those of you who aren't.

AQUARIUM

Duman Entertainment Centre, 4 Kabanbai Batyr Prospect, Almaty
Tel: 242 222
Open: daily, 10am–10pm

The Duman Entertainment Centre houses the furthest salt-water and shark-filled oceanarium from the sea anywhere in the world, as well as a 3D-cinema and a number of restaurants. Entrance to the oceanarium costs 2,000 tenge for foreigners.

EXCURSIONS AROUND ASTANA

Borovoye

Often called Little Switzerland, the Borovoye National Park is one of Northern Kazakhstan's most photographed attractions. Just three hours north of Astana, the park contains a number of lakes and wooded landscapes rich in flora and fauna. The region is known for its health-giving properties and a series of sanatoria and hotels on the lakes shores offer up therapies in addition to rest and relaxation.

Kokshetau

Possibly the birthplace of the domesticated horse, the area around Kokshetau is an area of outstanding natural beauty, home to mountains, hills, forests and rocky peaks broken up by small crystal-clear lakes. As in Korgalzhyn, the Ecotourism Information Resource Centre can organize homestays within three villages in the Kokshetau National Park, which is 60 kilometres southwest of Kokshetau and home to a unique mix of Siberian and Central Asian flora and fauna. A trip to Kokshetau is a good way to spend a healthy and relaxing weekend. Trips can be organized through the Ecotourism Information Resource Centre (see Almaty Play section) or you can contact the NGO Ekos at akmol-ekos@mail.kz (Russian only).

Korgalzhyn

Despite being under three hours from Astana and possessing a collection of birdlife that has recently attracted a nomination for UNESCO World Heritage site status, the Korgalzhyn area remains surprisingly unknown, even within Kazakhstan. Located at the crossroads of two migration routes, the vast wetland area is home to wolves, marmots and the rare Saiga antelope. However, it is the birds, and the pink flamingo in particular, that are the real attraction of this combination of virgin steppe and lakes. The area, most of which is protected as a National Nature Reserve, is home to the world's most northerly population of pink flamingos, one of over 300 species of birds and includes one of the largest wildfowl populations in Asia. Other notable residents include the Dalmatian pelican, the white-headed duck, a number of cranes and a variety of birds of prey.

Trips to Korgalzhyn can be organized through the Ecotourism Information Resource Centre (see Almaty Play section) or you can contact Ljudmila at the NGO Rodnik on OORodnik@mail.ru. Telephone 8 3163 72 10 43.

Malinovka

Malinovka is a small settlement to the west of Astana, which was home to 'Site 26' or ALZHIR – 'The Akmola Camp for Wives of Enemies of the Motherland'. Because Akmola played a major part in what Alexander Solzhenitsyn termed 'the gulag archipelago' (Solzhenitsyn himself was imprisoned in a gulag further east at Ekibastuz), it is well worth visiting this moving site just 30 minutes' drive from Astana. The small museum documents the history of the prison camp system in Northern Kazakhstan. The Avenue of Tears at the former entrance to the camp has metal plaques listing the prisoners' names, and the monuments at Malinovka are a moving tribute to the wives who were arrested during the Stalin era and imprisoned in the ALZHIR camp.

Any of the above excursions can be organized either independently or through the travel agents listed at the end of the Almaty Play section.

GOLF

Astana Golf Club, Karaganda Road, Karaganda Trassa
Tel: 297 526
Open: daily, 9am (8am Sat/Sun)–sunset

Opened in 2000, the soon to be 18-hole Astana Golf Club (the back nine holes will be ready in 2008) is an oasis of green in the middle of the steppe. Attracting Astana's top brass, including the President himself, the Astana Golf Club will cost 15,000 tenge a day in green fees once all 18 holes are in action. There is also a driving range adjacent to the clubhouse and it is possible to rent clubs, carts and even a caddy at the club. In addition, the clubhouse offers a sauna and a restaurant; a day spent here is a very pleasant escape from city life.

ICE SKATING

Ice City, Between Duman Entertainment Centre and the River Ishim, Central Park

Every year, between December and March, ice sculptors create an Ice City on Astana's Left Bank featuring replicas of some of the world's most famous buildings. Thus it becomes possible to walk among (and slide down and skate next to) the Parthenon, the Eiffel Tower, the Taj Mahal, Big Ben, the Pyramids of Giza and Astana's very own Baiterek without the inconvenience of intercontinental travel in between.

Ice Club, Eurasia Trade Centre, House 3, Microdistrict 2
Tel: 341 409
Open: daily, 10am–10pm

Located behind the Eurasia Trade Centre in Microdistrict 2, the Ice Club is a large skating rink costing 1,500 tenge for 75 minutes. The club also offers bowling from 1pm to 3am costing 3,500 tenge per hour for four people. Should you want to bowl in peace, you can hire a VIP bowling room for $300 for one hour, which can accommodate up to eight people.

Kazakhstan Sports Complex, 9 Munaytpasov St, Canalside, Almaty
Tel: 353 491 or 353 490
Open: daily, 10am–10pm

The ice rink at the Kazakhstan Sports Complex (located just off Ablai Khan when you cross the canal) opens from September to April and costs 700 tenge for one hour. There is also a large swimming pool where you can swim for 400 tenge an hour.

RACING

Altyn Taga Hippodrome, Rozhdestvenko Road
Tel: n/a

Astana's brand new hippodrome can hold up to 2,600 spectators and was opened in July 2007 to coincide with the tenth anniversary of Astana's capital status. Designed for racing and Kazakh traditional sports, various events take place in the Hippodrome throughout the summer months.

RIDING

Tulpar Horse Sports Club, Lesnaya Street, Koktal Microdistrict
Tel: 300 850

Located off the Astrakhan Trassa (road), Tulpar is a small horse farm and restaurant where it is possible to take riding lessons. Ring for up-to-date prices.

SKIING

Cross-country skiing

Much of northern Kazakhstan is classic Nordic skiing country – flat, with lots of snow for at least four months of winter once the snow falls in

November (or earlier). Cross-country skiing is popular among outdoors enthusiasts who often use the old wooden skis they've used for the past twenty years. However, it is wild skiing, finding your own routes and making your own tracks, with a minimum of provision.

Ishim River

In Astana people go skiing along the river in winter. You can rent passable skis and boots at a little lodge by the river in the main city park. It is next to the place where local people cut a hole in the ice and go for a bracing swim on weekend mornings – a good way, perhaps, to cool down after your skiing exertions.

SPAS & BATHS

Rixos Royal Spa, Rixos President Hotel, 7 1st Street, Almaty
Tel: 245 050   www.rixosastana.com
Rates: 3,900 tenge Mon–Fri; 6,500 tenge Sat–Sun

With its heart-shaped swimming pool, fitness club, Finnish sauna, Turkish *hammam*, solarium and three Thai masseuses, the Rixos Royal Spa is an oasis of calm and relaxation at the centre of Astana's Left Bank. It is well worth coming here if you have a free day and want to escape the noise and dirt associated with the construction of the new capital. A one-hour Thai massage will cost you 9,000 tenge and if you are feeling really indulgent you can order a Thai Sultan massage for 14,000 tenge, which will give you the unadulterated attention of two pairs of hands at once. We highly recommend it.

Sary Arka Baths, Sary Arka St (Korgalzhyn Trassa), Sary Arka
Tel: 798 100
Open: 10am (8am Sat/Sun)–10pm. Closed Mondays.

Modelled on Almaty's Arasan Banya, the newly opened (spring 2007) Sary Arka Baths is the perfect spot after a night of wining, dining and partying in Kazakhstan's capital. Indulge yourself in Sary Arka's Turkish *hammam* or traditional Russian *banya* and wash your sins away.

VIP Sauna Emir, Astana Park Hotel, Sary Arka Bridge, Central Park
Tel: 556 333

Hire out this swanky VIP sauna in the Astana Park Hotel (see Sleep) and you will be able to take advantage of a dazzling sauna with its very own gold and cream mosaic plunge pool, a crimson and tiled Moghul-style dining room and a dedicated billiards room upstairs, with – should you feel fatigued by the whole event – its very own adjacent bedroom. To make a night of it, order food and drinks from the hotel's in-house 'Chalet' restaurant. Price: 15,000 tenge per hour.

TENNIS

Tennis Courts, adjacent to Atameken Ethno Memorial Complex on Kabanbai Batyr, Central Park
Tel: 241 264

Open: daily from 6am in the summer

Tennis courts costs 800 tenge per hour in the open air, or 1,500 tenge per hour on the indoor court; lessons with a coach cost from 2,000 tenge per hour, plus the rent of the court.

Notes & Updates

CLIMATE

Kazakhstan has an extreme continental climate, meaning the summers are very hot, and the winters are very cold. Winter, which can start at any time from mid-October onwards, often lasts until late April, when the buds and leaves on the trees develop seemingly overnight. In the winter, you will find that Almaty is milder than Astana, with temperatures generally just below zero, although they occasionally plummet to −10 or −15°C. Almaty, with its many trees, is magical when the snow falls. In Astana, temperatures are lower, and routinely fall as low as −30°C, a fact compounded by windchill. Conversely, summer temperatures, especially in July and August, can reach 35°C. If you want to do any trekking in the mountains around Almaty, the season lasts from June to mid–September. Autumn is wonderful (September and October) when the bazaars are stocked full of local fruits and the leaves on Almaty's many trees turn gold.

DANGERS

Almaty and Astana are friendly towns and walking around on your own is rarely a problem. That said it is always best to take precautions and not to walk in dark places alone. Emergency service telephone numbers are: Fire Brigade – 01, Police – 02, Ambulance – 03.

MONEY

The Kazakh unit of currency is called the tenge and the exchange rate is roughly £1 = 240 tenge, $1 = 122 tenge and €1 = 170 tenge. ATM machines generally dispense tenge, although certain machines dispense dollars too. It is occasionally possible to pay in dollars, but the tenge is the legal unit of currency. If you do have dollars, ensure they are in good condition as currency exchange cashiers occasionally reject damaged notes. Credit cards are accepted at most places although it is not uncommon for the credit card terminal to be out of order.

STEPPE MAGAZINE

If you're interested in learning more about the art, culture, history and people of Central Asia why not check out Steppe – Central Asia's first English-language, coffee table magazine. Published twice a year with glossy photo essays and detailed *info...*

articles, Steppe is the perfect reading companion for your trip to the steppe. Look for Steppe at Ramstore and the InterContinental and Hyatt bookstores (in Almaty) and the Rixos bookstore in Astana, or check out www.steppemagazine.com.

TAXIS

Taxis on call are reliable and safe, but they'll charge a minimum of 1,500 tenge. In Almaty, call 002 or 058; in Astana, call 22 22 22 or 39 79 79 (no English spoken). You can also flag down gypsy taxis or private cars in the street starting from 300 tenge to go anywhere in the city. However, take care, especially at night, and do not get into a car that has more than one person already in it. In Astana, taxis tend to be a bit more expensive, so be prepared to pay from 500 tenge.

TELEPHONES

The country code for Kazakhstan is +7. The Almaty city code is 7272 and the Astana city code is 7172. If you are dialling out of town, or to a mobile, put an 8 in front of the code.

TIPPING

It is worth bearing in mind that the majority of restaurants will include a 10% service charge at the end of your bill. Do check, though, especially if the service has been good as many waiters and waitresses are students who are trying to pay their way through college, and don't be shy to tip on top if you are satisfied. A similar percentage tip works well for guides and drivers who have done a good job.

VISAS

It is now possible to get a one-month single entry private, business or tourist visa for Kazakhstan without needing a letter of invitation. Instead, you need to present a letter of introduction explaining the purpose of your visit, and take this, with forms, photos, passport and money, to your local consulate.

index